BIMETRICAL PSALTER

D.R. OLSON

Copyright ©2025 by Douglas Robert Olson
All rights reserved.
ISBN: 978-1-7358126-4-9

Preface

This book contains a bimetrical version of each psalm in the Bible. In most of the psalms of this version, each stanza follows one of two meters. A dot at the left of its first line marks a stanza in the second meter, and the absence of such a dot indicates a stanza in the first. In several psalms, all stanzas follow the same meter. The appendix at the back of the book provides a list of the meters for each psalm and a list of the psalms in each meter followed.

In composing this psalter, I have borrowed heavily from the King James Version of the psalms.

D.R. Olson
12 November 2024

Contents

Book I 1

Book II 65

Book III 115

Book IV 149

Book V 177

Appendix 259

Book I

Psalm 1

Blessed is the man that in
the counsel of the wicked doth not walk,
nor standeth in the way of them that sin,
nor sitteth in the seat of them that mock.

[2] But in YAHWEH's law is his delight;
and in his law he meditateth day and night.

[3] And he shall be like a tree with root
by streams of water, bearing in his time his fruit;

and his leaf shall not decay;
and whatsoever doeth he shall thrive.
[4] The wicked are not so: but rather they
are like the chaff which wind away doth drive.

[5] Therefore in the judgment shall not stand
the wicked, neither sinners in the just ones' band.

[6] For the LORD doth know the just ones' way:
the way, though, of the wicked ones shall go astray.

Psalm 2

Why do the heathen clamor, and
the people vainly meditate?
²The kings of earth dispose themselves,
the rulers, too, deliberate

unitedly, against the LORD
and his anointed, saying thus,
³Asunder let us break their bands,
and cast away their cords from us.

⁴The one that sitteth in the heav'ns
shall laugh: the Lord shall them deride.
⁵Then he in wrath shall speak to them,
and make in ire them terrified.

⁶Yet I've upon my holy hill
of Zion set my king. ⁷Avow
will I the statute of the LORD:
said he to me, My Son art thou;

this day have I begotten thee.
⁸Request of me, and I'll legate
the heathen for thine heritance,
and ends of earth for thine estate.

⁹With a rod of iron thou shalt shatter them;
like a potter's vessel thou shalt scatter them.

¹⁰And so, ye kings, be wise now: ye
that judge the earth, take discipline.
¹¹In terror serve JEHOVAH, and
rejoice with trembling.¹²Kiss the Son,

lest anger he, and from the way
ye perish, when his wrath doth burn
but little. Bless'd are all of they
that unto him for refuge turn.

Psalm 3

· Lord, how they're multiplied that vex me! They
are many that against me rise. ²Declare
ones many of my soul, For him
no deliverance in God is there.　　　　　*Selah.*

· ³But thou, O Yahweh, art a shield for me;
my glory, and the lifter of my head.
⁴I cried to Yahweh with my voice,
and he heard me from his hill sacred.　　*Selah.*

· ⁵I laid me down and slept; awaked I; for
the Lord sustained me. ⁶I'll not be afraid
of myriads of people, that
round about against me are arrayed.

· ⁷Arise, O Yahweh; save me, O my God:
for thou hast smitten all them that me hate
upon the cheek bone; broken hast
thou the teeth of persons reprobate.

⁸Belongeth to the Lord salvation:
thy blessing is upon thy nation.　　　　*Selah.*

Psalm 4

¹ Hear me when I call, O God of my righteousness:
thou hast given me relief when I was in distress;

have upon me mercy, also hear my prayer.
²O ye sons of men, how long will my
glory ye turn into ignominy? How
long will love ye vanity, and seek for a lie?   *Selah.*

³Know, though, that the Lord hath set apart him that's
godly for himself: Jehovah will
hear my call to him. ⁴Be moved, and do not sin:
with your heart commune upon your bed, and be still.
                                                                  Selah.
⁵Offer ye the sacrifice of righteousness;
trust, too, in Jehovah. ⁶Numerous
be the ones that say, Who'll show us any good?
Lift thou up the light, Lord, of thy face upon us.

⁷In my heart thou hast put gladness, more than in
times their corn and wine was multiplied.
⁸I'll both lay me down in peace, and slumber: for
thou alone, Lord, makest me in safety abide.

Psalm 5

Jehovah, give thou ear unto my words;
consider thou my meditation. ²Pay
heed unto the bellow of my cry,
my King and God: for I to thee will pray.

³At break of day my voice,
Lord, thou shalt hear;
at break of day will I direct
my prayer to thee, and up will peer.

⁴For thou art not a God that hath delight
in wrong: and evil shan't abide with thee.
⁵Foolish ones shall stand not in thy sight:
thou hatest all who work iniquity.

⁶The liars thou shalt cause to die: the Lord
will loathe the man of blood and treachery.
⁷As for me, though, I will come into
thy house in vastness of thy clemency:

and in thy fear will worship I toward
thy holy temple. ⁸Lead me, Lord, in thy
righteousness by reason of my foes;
before thy face, my way do rectify.

⁹Because there's in their mouth no faithfulness,
their inward part's itself calamity,
and their throat's an open sepulchre;
they with their tongue distribute flattery.

¹⁰Destroy thou them, O God, and let them fall
by their own counsels; drive thou them away
in the multitude of their misdeeds;
because against thee have rebellèd they.

¹¹But let all those that put
in thee their trust
rejoice: let them forever shout
for joy, for thou defend them dost:

moreover let the ones that love thy name
in thee be joyful. ¹²For the righteous being,
O Jehovah, thou wilt bless; as with
a shield, with favor thou wilt him enring.

Psalm 6

¹O Jehovah, in thy wrath rebuke me not,
neither in thy hot displeasure me upbraid.
²Have mercy on me, Lord; for I am weak: O Lord,
heal me; for my bones, they are dismayed.

³My soul is also sorely vexed:
but thou, Jehovah, how
long? ⁴Return, O Lord, my soul deliver: for
thy lovingkindness' sake, oh save me thou.

⁵For there's no memorial of thee in death:
who shall praise thee in the grave? ⁶Fatigued am I
with groaning; all the night I make my bed to swim;
with my tears my couch I liquefy.

⁷Wasted is mine eye because of anguish; it
waxeth old because of all my vexers. ⁸All
ye workers of iniquity, depart from me;
for the Lord hath heard my tearful bawl.

⁹The Lord hath heard my plea; my prayer
Jehovah will embrace.
¹⁰Let ashamed and sorely vexed be all my foes:
let them return and forthwith feel disgrace.

Psalm 7

O my God JEHOVAH, I
put my trust in thee:
save thou me from all who chase
me, and rescue me:

²lest to pieces tear my soul
like a lion he,
rending, while to rescue there
is no entity.

³LORD my God, if I have done this; if
there be iniquity
in my hands; ⁴if evil I have paid
to him that was at peace with me;
(yea, I have delivered him that is
without a cause mine enemy:)

⁵let the enemy pursue my soul,
and overtake it; yea,
let him trample to the ground my life,
and in the dust mine honor lay.   *Selah.*

⁶Rise, LORD, in thine anger, lift thyself
against the angry blast
of my foes: and rouse thyself for me;
a judgment thou commanded hast.

⁷So shall the assembly of
peoples compass thee:
therefore, for their sakes return
to sublimity.

⁸Judge the peoples shall JEHOVAH: O
JEHOVAH, judge thou me
as unto my righteousness and mine
integrity that is in me.

⁹Let the wickedness of wicked ones
please come to an arrest;
stablish, though, the just one: for the hearts
and reins the righteous God doth test.

¹⁰My protection is of God, which doth
   the upright-hearted save.
¹¹God doth judge the righteous one, and God
   is angry daily with the knave.

¹²If he turn not, he will whet his sword;
   his bow hath bended he,
   and prepared it. ¹³And he hath prepared
   for him the deadly weaponry;

 fabricateth he his arrows for
   the persecutors. ¹⁴See,
   he doth writhe with sin, and hath conceived
   travail, and gendered falsity.

¹⁵Excavated he a pit,
   and it he did spade,
   and is fallen into the
   very ditch he made.

¹⁶On his head his devilry
   shall return, and down
   shall his dealing violent
   come on his own crown.

¹⁷As unto his righteousness,
   praise the Lord will I:
   and I'll sing unto the name
   of the Lord most high.

Psalm 8

· ¹Lord our Lord, how great in all the earth is thy
name! Who hast thy glory set above the sky.

²From the mouth of babes and sucklings hast
ordained thou strength by reason of thy foes,
so that thou mightest make the enemy
and avenger to repose.

· ³When thy heavens I behold, thy fingers' deed,
moon as well as stars, the which thou hast decreed;

· ⁴what is man, that in thy mind him thou dost bear?
And the son of man, that thou for him dost care?

· ⁵For just lower than the gods thou hast him downed,
and with weightiness and honor hast him crowned.

⁶Over the creations of thy hands,
thou gavest him dominion; thou beneath
his feet hast put all things:⁷ all sheep and kine,
yea, as well the beasts of heath;

⁸fowl of air, and fish of sea, and all
that passeth through the pathways of the sea.
⁹O Lord our Lord, how excellent is thy
name in earth's entirety!

Psalm 9

¹ I will praise thee, Lord, with all of my heart;
I will all thy marvelous works proclaim.
²I will be joyful and exult in thee:
I will sing, thou One Supreme, to thy name.

³When mine enemies are turned to the rear,
they shall fall and perish before thy sight.
⁴Because thou hast maintained my right and cause;
in the throne thou satest, one judging right.

⁵Thou hast rebuked the heathen and
the wicked one destroyed,
ever and forever hast their
name thou rendered void.

⁶O thou enemy, destructions are come
to a termination perpetual:
thou hast eradicated cities, too;
perished with them is their memorial.

⁷But Jehovah shall endure evermore:
stablished for the judgment his throne hath he.
⁸And he shall judge the world in righteousness,
he shall rule the people with equity.

⁹And the Lord will be the oppressed's retreat,
a retreat in times of adversity.
¹⁰They'll trust in thee that know thy name: for thou,
Lord, hast not left them that inquire of thee.

¹¹To the Lord, which dwelleth in Zion, sing:
in the populace, of his doings speak.
¹²For he that seeketh blood rememb'reth them:
he forgetteth not the cry of the meek.

¹³O Jehovah, mercy upon me have;
see mine ignominy which suffer I
of persons that detest me, O thou that
from the gates of death me upliftest high:

¹⁴that I may show forth all thy praise
in Zion's daughter's gates:
I, in the deliverance of
thee, will jubilate.

¹⁵The heathen are sunk down in the
corruption that they wrought:
in the net which they concealed
their own foot is caught.

¹⁶The Lord is known by judgment which
he doth administrate:
in the work of his own hands is
snared the reprobate.   *Higgaion. Selah.*

¹⁷The ungodly shall be turned into hell;
all the nations that forget God, too. ¹⁸For
the needy shall not alway be forgot:
nor forever fail the hope of the poor.

¹⁹Rise, Jehovah; do not let man prevail:
let the heathen be adjudged in thy ken.
²⁰Them put in fear, Jehovah, so that may
nations know themselves to be merely men. *Selah.*

Psalm 10

[1] Why dost stand thou far away, LORD? Why dost thou
hide thyself in seasons of adversity?
[2] The wicked doth in pride pursue the poor:
in schemes they've plotted let them taken be.

[3] For the wicked boasteth of his heart's desire;
blesseth he the greedy, whom the LORD doth hate.
[4] According to his countenance's pride,
the wicked one will not investigate:

God is not in all his thoughts.
[5] His ways are all the time profane;
thy judgments are on high, beyond his sight:
he'll over all his foes dominion gain.

[6] In his heart hath said he, I shall not be moved:
for I never shall be in adversity.
[7] His mouth is full of cursing, guile, and fraud:
beneath his tongue is toil and vanity.

[8] In the blinds of villages
he sitteth: in the secret lies
doth murder he the innocent: against
the pauper privily are set his eyes.

[9] As a lion in his den,
in wait he lieth secretly:
to catch the poor he lurketh: he doth catch
the poor, when in his net him draweth he.

[10] He is shattered, also humbleth he himself,
that the poor may fall beneath his strong ones. [11] He
hath said within his heart, God hath forgot:
his face he hideth; he will never see.

[12] Rise, O LORD; O God, uplift
thy hand: forget thou not the meek.
[13] Why doth the wicked person spurn God? He
hath said within his heart, Thou wilt not seek.

[14] Thou hast seen; for thou beholdest mischief and
provocation, to it with thy hand redress:
the poor committeth unto thee himself;
thou art the helper of the fatherless.

¹⁵·Break the wicked and the evil person's arm:
  seek thou out his wickedness till none thou find.
¹⁶·The LORD is King from old and evermore:
  the heathen from his land are quite declined.

¹⁷·Thou hast heard the wish, LORD, of the humble: thou
  wilt prepare their heart and cause thine ear to hear:
¹⁸ to judge the orphan and oppressed one, that
  the man of earth may cause no longer fear.

Psalm 11

In Jehovah trust I: how say ye
to my soul, O bird, unto your mountain flee?

²For, behold, their bow the wicked bend,
on the string their arrow they prepare to send,

that at the upright ones in heart
they may in darkness shoot.
³If the foundations be destroyed,
what can the righteous do?

⁴The Lord is in his holy hall;
his throne is in the sky:
the progeny of men his eyes
behold and eyelids try.

⁵The Lord doth try the righteous one
and person reprobate;
but him that loveth violence,
he his own soul doth hate.

⁶Upon the wicked, snares of fire
and brimstone shall he rain,
and scorching wind: unto their cup
this portion shall pertain.

⁷For the Lord is righteous; loveth he
righteousness; his face the upright one doth see.

Psalm 12

$\cdot$ Help, LORD; for the godly man doth terminate;
because among the sons of men the faithful dissipate.

$\cdot$ ²Ev'ryone discusseth falsehood with his mate:
with lips of flattery and with a double heart they prate.

³The LORD shall sever all the lips of flattery,
and tongue that speaketh things imperious:
⁴who've boasted, With our tongue will we prevail;
our lips are ours: who's master over us?

⁵Because of the oppression of the humble ones,
because of sighing of the persons poor,
I'll now arise, doth say the LORD, I'll set
him in the safety that he panteth for.

$\cdot$ ⁶YAHWEH's words are sayings pure: as silver tried
within an earthen furnace, seven times repurified.

⁷O YAHWEH, thou shalt keep them, us thou shalt preserve
for ever from this generation. ⁸Prowl
on ev'ry side do the ungodly ones,
when elevated are the men most foul.

Psalm 13

[1] How long, O Lord, wilt thou forget me? Evermore?
How long wilt thou conceal thy face from me?
[2] How long shall take I counsel in my soul,
having daily in my heart despondency?
How long shall mine opponent be exalted over me?

[3] Regard and answer me, O Lord my God:
mine eyes enlighten, lest the sleep of death I sleep;
[4] lest should say mine enemy, I've mastered him;
when I'm moved my troublers in elation leap.

[5] But I have trusted in thy steadfast love;
in thy deliverance my heart shall leap with glee.
[6] I will sing unto the Lord, because he hath
bountifully showered benefits on me.

Psalm 14

The fool hath said within his heart, There's no
God. They are corrupt, they've done
works abominable, there
is that doeth good not one.

²From heaven downward looked the Lord upon
sons of men, in order to
see if any understood,
or did after God pursue.

³Aside are gone them all, they are become
all together filthy: none
is who executeth good,
no, there is not even one.

⁴Are all who work iniquity without
knowledge? Who devour my
people as they gobble bread,
and to Yahweh do not cry.

⁵They there had terror great: for God's in the
generation of the just.
⁶Ye have shamed the plan of the
poor, for Yahweh is his trust.

⁷Oh that out of Zion were
Israel's salvation come!
When the Lord doth turn his clan's captivity,
Jacob shall rejoice, and Israel shall be gleesome.

Psalm 15

[1] LORD, who shall abide within thy tabernacle?
In thy holy mountain who shall dwell?
[2] He that walketh uprightly, and worketh righteousness,
and the truth he in his heart doth tell.

[3] He with his tongue calumniateth not,
doeth he no evil to his peer,
nor taketh up reproach
against his neighbor near.

[4] The vile person in his eyes is scorned;
but he honoreth the ones that fear
the LORD. He sweareth to
his hurt, and doth not veer.

[5] He giveth not his coin to usury,
nor against the innocent doth take
reward. The doer of
these things shall never shake.

Psalm 16

O God, preserve me: for unto
thee for refuge do I dart.
²O my soul, unto J<small>EHOVAH</small> thou
hast confessed, My Lord thou art:

to thee my goodness reacheth not;
³to the saints that are in the
earth and to the excellent: in them's
my delight entirely.

⁴Multiplied shall be the sorrows of the ones
that unto another god do hasten: their
libatory offerings of blood I'll not
pour, and on my lips their names I will not bear.

⁵Y<small>AHWEH</small> is the portion of my heritance
and my cup: thou art the one that holdest my
lot. ⁶In pleasant places are to me the lines
fallen; yea, a goodly heritage have I.

⁷I will bless the L<small>ORD</small>, who hath me counseled: my
reins instruct me also in the times of night.
⁸I have set the L<small>ORD</small> before me constantly:
I shall not be moved for he is at my right.

⁹Thus my heart is glad, rejoiceth also my
glory: yea, my flesh shall rest in hope. ¹⁰For not
leave my soul in Hades wilt thou; neither wilt
thou allow thy Holy One to witness rot.

¹¹The path of life thou wilt me show:
with thy face satiety
of rejoicing is; at thy right hand
are delights eternally.

Psalm 17

· Hear the right, O LORD, attend thou to my cry,
hearken to my prayer, not out of lips of treachery.
²From thy face let forth my sentence come; let thine
eyes behold the things of equity.

³Thou hast assayed my heart; at night hast
visited me thou; refined
me thou hast, and nothing shalt thou find; that my
mouth shall not transgress I have designed.

· ⁴In concern of works of men, by word of thy
lips, from paths of the destroyer I have guarded me.
⁵In thy paths uphold my goings, so that my
footsteps slip not. ⁶I have called on thee,

· for thou, God, wilt hear me: bend thine ear to me,
hear mine utterance. ⁷Thy wondrous mercies advertise,
thou that savest them which at thy right hand take
refuge from those that against them rise.

· ⁸Keep me as the apple of the eye, me hide
in the shadow of thy wings, ⁹from wicked persons that
spoil me, from my deadly enemies, who me
compass. ¹⁰They're inclosed in their own fat:

their mouth doth speak in pride. ¹¹Encompassed
us now in our steps have they:
they have set their eyes to cast me to the earth;
¹²like a lion greedy of his prey,

and as a lion cub in secret
places lurking. ¹³Rise, O LORD,
meet him, cast him down: deliver thou my soul
from the wicked one, which is thy sword:

¹⁴from men which are thy hand, O LORD, from
worldly men, which in this life
have their allocation, and whose belly thou
with thy hidden treasure fillest rife:

· they are full of children, and they leave the rest
of their substance to their babes. ¹⁵But I, in rectitude
I will see thy face: I shall be sated, when
I awake, with thy similitude.

Psalm 18

· I will love thee, Lord, my strength. ²The Lord's my rock,
my fortress and deliverer, moreover; my
God, my strength, in whom I'll trust; my shield, and
horn of my salvation, and my tower high.

· ³I will call upon the Lord, who's worthy to
be praised: so from mine enemies I saved shall be.
⁴Agonies of death encompassed me, and
torrents of ungodly men affrighted me.

⁵Agonies of hell encompassed me
round about: me snares of death defied.
⁶I, in mine affliction, called upon
Yahweh, and unto my God I cried:

· heard my voice he from his temple, and my cry
before him came into his ears. ⁷Then agitate
and convulse the earth did; hills' foundations
also moved and shook, because he was irate.

⁸From his nostrils there ascended smoke,
also from his mouth devoured flame:
by it were ignited coals. ⁹And he
bowed the heavens, also down he came:

· and beneath his feet was darkness. ¹⁰And he rode
upon a cherub, and did fly: indeed, apace
he did fly upon the wings of wind. ¹¹And
he established darkness for his secret place;

his pavilion round about him were
waters dark and massive clouds in air.
¹²At the brightness that before him was,
passed his clouds with hail and coals aflare.

· ¹³Yahweh also thundered in the heavens, and
the Highest gave his voice with hail and coals alit.
¹⁴Yea, he sent his arrows, and them scattered;
lightnings shot he, too; them did he discomfit.

¹⁵Then the streams of waters were beheld,
and the world's foundations were exposed
at thy reprimand, Lord, at the blast
of the breath of nostrils of thy nose.

$\cdot^{16}$From above he sent, he took me, me he drew
from out of many waters.^{17}He delivered me
from my mighty foe, and from the ones which
hated me: because they were too strong for me.

$\cdot^{18}$In the day of my calamity did they
prevent me: but the Lord was my support.^{19}And he
brought me forth into a roomy place; me
he delivered, for in me delighted he.

^{20}Me the Lord rewarded as to my
righteousness; to me he hath restored
as unto the cleanness of my hands.
^{21}For I've kept the courses of the Lord,

· and I have not wickedly departed from
my Deity.^{22}For all his judgments were before
me, and put I not away from me his
statutes.^{23}I was whole before him furthermore,

· and I kept myself from mine iniquity.
^{24}The Lord hath recompensed me in accord with my
righteousness in consequence, according
to the cleanness of my hands before his eye.

·^{25}With the kind thyself wilt thou show kind; and with
an upright man thyself wilt thou show absolute;
^{26}with the pure thyself wilt thou show pure; and
with the froward thou wilt show thyself astute.

^{27}For the humble people thou wilt save;
but the haughty looks thou wilt depress.
^{28}For my candle thou wilt light: my God
Yahweh will illume my gloominess.

·^{29}For by thee have run I through a troop; and by
my God have leaped I o'er a wall.^{30}This Deity!
Perfect is his way: refined is Yahweh's
word: to all that trust in him a shield is he.

^{31}For apart from Yahweh who is God?
Or who is a rock except our God?
^{32}It is God that girdeth me with strength,
also maketh he my way unflawed.

³³Maketh he my feet like those of hinds,
setteth he me on my heights also.
³⁴Teacheth he my hands to war, so that
by mine arms is bent a brazen bow.

³⁵Thou to me hast also given the
shield of thy salvation: also thy
right hand hath upholden me, and thy
gentleness hath made me multiply.

³⁶Thou hast made my steps beneath me wide;
slipped not then my feet. ³⁷My foes I've chased,
and have overtaken them, and I
turned not back until they were laid waste.

³⁸I have wounded them so that they could
not arise: beneath my feet are they
fallen down. ³⁹Thou hast with valiance
also girded me unto the fray:

under me thou hast subdued those that
up against me rose. ⁴⁰Thou hast as well
given unto me the necks of my
foes; so that my haters I might fell.

⁴¹Cried they out, but there was none to save them: yea,
to YAHWEH, but to them he granted no reply.
⁴²Then I beat them small as dust before the
wind: as dirt in roadways, cast them out did I.

⁴³From the strivings of the people hast
thou delivered me; the head of the
heathen thou hast made me also: a
people I have known not shall serve me.

⁴⁴When they hear of me, they shall obey
me: submit shall foreigners to me.
⁴⁵Foreigners shall fade away and shall
out of their enclosures frightened be.

⁴⁶YAHWEH liveth; blessèd be my rock;
let the God of my salvation be
lifted high. ⁴⁷This God's the being who
granteth acts of vengeance unto me,

and subdueth peoples under me.
[48]From my foes delivereth me he:
furthermore, above the persons that
rise against me, thou upliftest me:

from the man of violence thou hast
me delivered.[49]Therefore I'll acclaim
thee, O LORD, among the heathen, and
praises will I sing unto thy name.

[50]Great deliverance unto his king
giveth he; and showeth mercy he
to his one anointed, David, and
his descendants for eternity.

Psalm 19

· The heavens numerate God's glory; his
handiwork the firmament doth also tell.
²Day to day doth utter speech,
knowledge night to night doth show as well.

³There's no speech nor language; heard is
not their voice. ⁴Their line's
gone through all the earth, their sayings
to the world's confines.

· A tabernacle hath he set in them
for the sun,⁵ which, as a bridegroom coming out
of his chamber, doth rejoice
as a mighty man to run a route.

⁶From the end of heaven is his
exit, and his beat
to its ends: and there is nothing
hidden from its heat.

⁷Perfect is the law of YAHWEH,
turning back the soul:
sure is YAHWEH's testimony,
making wise the dull.

⁸Statutes of the LORD are straight, the
heart embrightening;
the command of YAHWEH's pure, the
eyes enlightening.

⁹Terror of the LORD is clean, for
ever standing tight;
judgments of the LORD are true and
altogether right.

¹⁰They are more to be desired than
gold, indeed, than much
fine gold: sweeter, too, than honey
and the comb of such.

·¹¹Moreover by them is thy servant warned:
also in their keeping there's abundant yield.
¹²His mistakes who can discern?
Cleanse thou me from trespasses concealed.

¹³Restrain thy servant from presumptuous sins
also; over me let not them dominate:
then shall I be upright, and
innocent from the transgression great.

¹⁴Let my mouth's discourses, and my
heart's reflection, be
pleasing in thy sight, Lord, strength and
ransomer of me.

Psalm 20

Y<small>AHWEH</small> hear thee in the day
of adversity;
may the name of Jacob's God
be defense for thee;

²from the sanctuary send thee
help, and out of Zion thee uphold;
³remember all thine offerings,
and accept as fat thine off'ring coaled.
                                        Selah.
⁴Grant thee as to thine own heart,
furthermore fulfil
all thy counsel. ⁵Joy in thy
victory we will,

and our banners, in the name
of our God, we will
set up: thy petitions all
may the L<small>ORD</small> fulfil.

⁶Now I know that Y<small>AHWEH</small> saveth
his anointed; answer him will he
with saving strength of his right hand
from the heaven of his sanctity.

⁷Some trust in the chariot,
others in the horse:
but the name of Y<small>AHWEH</small> our
God will we endorse.

⁸They are bended down and fallen:
we are risen, though, and stand we tall.
⁹O Y<small>AHWEH</small>, save thou: let the king
answer us the day in which we call.

Psalm 21

1. In thy fortitude, O Lord, the king shall
   gladden; and he shall rejoice in thy salvation how
   much! [2] His heart's desire thou hast him given,
   and his lips' request hast not withholden thou.   *Selah.*

[3] For thou meetest him with goodly blessings:
   on his head a crown of purest gold thou settest. [4] He
   asked for life of thee, thou gavest it him,
   length of days for ever to eternity.

[5] Great his glory is in thy salvation:
   honor and magnificence hast thou upon him laid.
   [6] For thou hast ordained him bless'd for ever:
   with thy presence very glad hast thou him made.

[7] For the king confideth in the Lord, and
   through the mercy of the Highest, shaken shan't he be.
   [8] All thine enemies thy hand shall find: thy
   right hand shall encounter those with hate for thee.

[9] Thou shalt make them as a fiery oven
   in the season of thine ire:
   in his wrath the Lord shall swallow up them,
   and devour them shall the fire.

[10] Thou shalt extirpate their fruit from earth, and
   from among the sons of men thou shalt destroy their seed.
   [11] For against thee they intended evil:
   they devised a wicked scheme; they'll not succeed.

[12] Therefore thou shalt make them turn their back, when
   thou shalt make thine arrows ready on thy bowstrings, drawn
   at their face. [13] Be thou exalted, Lord, in
   thine own strength: so will we sing and praise thy brawn.

Psalm 22

¹ My God, my God, why hast thou forsaken me?
Far from helping me are words of my lament.
² O my God, I cry by day, but hearest not
thou; and in the night, and I'm not reticent.

³ But thou art holy, O thou inhabiter
of the songs of praise of Israel. ⁴ Confide
did our fathers in thee: they confided, and
them thou didst deliver. ⁵ Unto thee they cried,

and they were rescued: trusted they
in thee, and they were not demoralized.
⁶ But I'm a worm, and not a man;
a reproach of men, and of the folk despised.

⁷ My viewers all laugh at me in scorn: they shoot
out the lip, they shake the head, remarking, ⁸ He
trusted on the LORD that he'd deliver him:
let him save him, for in him delighted he.

⁹ But thou art the agent of my breaking forth
from the matrix: thou didst make me hopeful when
on my mother's breasts. ¹⁰ On thee was cast I from
womb: thou art my God from mother's abdomen.

¹¹ Be not thou far from me; for near
is trouble; for there's no one to abet.
¹² Encompassed me have many bulls:
round have mighty bulls of Bashan me beset.

¹³ They gaped upon me with their mouths,
a lion that doth raven and doth roar.
¹⁴ Like water, I am pourèd out;
all my bones are in disjunction furthermore:

my heart is like wax; it's melted in the midst
of my bowels. ¹⁵ Like the fragment of a pot,
dried up is my strength; my tongue doth cleave to my
jaws; and to the dust of death thou hast me brought.

¹⁶ For dogs have compassed me: inclosed
me have the evildoers' company:
they pierced my hands and feet. ¹⁷ I may
tally all my bones: they look and stare at me.

¹⁸They part my clothes among themselves,
and for my vesture cast they lots.¹⁹But be,
O Yahweh, not thou far from me:
O my power, hasten thee to succour me.

²⁰Deliver from the sword my soul;
my darling from the mongrel's potency.
²¹Release me from the lion's mouth:
for thou from the oxen's horns hast answered me.

²²Unto my brethren I will declare thy name:
in the middle of the congregation I
will thee praise.²³Ye fearers of the Lord, him praise;
all of ye of Jacob's seed, him glorify;

and fear him, all ye the seed of Israel.
²⁴For he hath not scorned nor loathed the misery
of the pauper, nor hath hid his face from him;
rather, when to him he shouted, hearkened he.

²⁵My praise in the great assembly shall be of
thee: before his fearers I my vows will pay.
²⁶Eat shall meek ones, and be sated: praise the Lord
shall his seekers out: your heart shall live alway.

²⁷All ends of earth shall remember and return
to the Lord: and all the nations' clans before
thee shall worship.²⁸For the kingdom is the Lord's:
and among the nations he's the governor.

²⁹The fat ones all upon the earth
shall eat and worship: all of them that dive
to dust shall bow before his face:
even he who cannot keep his soul alive.

³⁰A seed shall serve him; accounted to the Lord
to the generation coming shall it be.
³¹They shall come, and shall declare his righteousness
to a people who'll be born, that done hath he.

Psalm 23

The L ORD is my shepherd; I'll not want.
²Me he maketh to lie down in pastures green:
by the waters still he leadeth me.
³He restoreth my being:

he leadeth me in the righteous paths
for his name's account. ⁴Yea, though I walk through the
valley of death's shadow, I'll not fear
evil: for thou art with me;

thy rod and thy staff they comfort me.
⁵In the presence of mine enemies dost spread
thou in front of me a table: with
oil anointest thou my head;

my cup runneth over. ⁶Goodness and
mercy surely shall pursue me all the days
of my life: and I will dwell in the
house of Y AHWEH for always.

Psalm 24

The earth is to Jehovah, and its fulness;
the world, and the persons that within it dwell.
²For he hath founded it upon the seas,
on the floods he stablished it as well.

³Who shall ascend into the mountain of the Lord?
Or who shall stand within his holy station? ⁴He
with guiltless hands and heart sincere; who hath not raised
his soul unto vanity, nor sworn deceitfully.

⁵He shall receive the blessing from Jehovah,
and justice from the God of his salvation, too.
⁶This is the generation, Jacob, of
them that seek him, that thy face pursue.   *Selah.*

⁷Uplift your heads, ye gates; and be ye lifted up,
ye doors eternal; and the King of majesty
shall enter in. ⁸Who is this King of majesty?
The Lord strong and stout, the Lord in battle masterly.

⁹Uplift your heads, ye portals; even lift them up,
ye doors eternal; and the King of majesty
shall enter in. ¹⁰Who is this King of majesty?
Jehovah of hosts, the King of majesty is he.   *Selah.*

Psalm 25

To thee, O Lord, I lift up my
soul. ²My God, I put my trust in thee:
let me not be shamed, let mine
enemies not triumph over me.

·³Yea, let none of them that wait on thee be shamed:
let them which transgress for nought confounded be.
⁴Make me know thy ways, O Lord; thy paths me teach.
⁵Lead me in thy truth, and teach thou me:

· for thou art the God of my salvation; on
thee I tarry all the day.⁶Recall, Lord, thy
tender mercies and thy lovingkindnesses;
for they've ever been from times gone by.

⁷Remember not the sins of my
youth, nor my transgressions: in accord
with thy mercy, bring to mind
thou me for thy goodness' sake, O Lord.

⁸The Lord is good and upright: thus
will direct he sinners in the way.
⁹He'll in judgment guide the meek:
also he will teach the meek his way.

·¹⁰All of Yahweh's paths are lovingkindness and
truth to such as keep his covenant and his
testimonies.¹¹For thy name's account, O Lord,
pardon mine offense; for great it is.

¹²What man is fearer of the Lord?
In the way he'll choose he'll edify
him.¹³His soul shall dwell at ease;
and the earth his seed shall occupy.

·¹⁴Yahweh's secret is with them that fear him; and
unto them his covenant he'll manifest.
¹⁵Ever are mine eyes toward the Lord; because
from the net my feet he forth shall wrest.

·¹⁶Turn thee unto me, and mercy have upon
me; for I am desolate and suffering.
¹⁷Widened are the tribulations of my heart:
out of mine adversities, me bring.

[18] Look on mine affliction and my pain; and all
of my sins forgive. [19] Behold my foes; for they
increase; and with cruel hatred they me hate.
[20] Keep my soul, and snatch thou me away:

· let me not be shamed; because in thee my trust
put I. [21] Let integrity and uprightness
guard me; for I wait on thee. [22] O God, redeem
Israel from all of his distress.

Psalm 26

^{1} Judge me, LORD; for I have walked in mine integrity:
in the LORD have also trusted I;
thus I shall not slide. ^{2} Examine me, O LORD,
prove me, too; my reins and heart do try.

^{3} For thy mercy is before mine eyes:
in thy truth I've walked also.
^{4} I've not sat with persons vain, nor in
with dissemblers will I go.

^{5} The assembly of the evildoers I have loathed;
and I'll sit not with the wicked horde.
^{6} I will wash my hands in innocency: and
I will go around thine altar, LORD:

^{7} so that I may publish with the voice of giving thanks,
and of all thy wondrous doings tell.
^{8} I have loved the domicile, LORD, of thy house,
and the place where doth thine honor dwell.

^{9} Gather not with sinners thou my soul,
nor with bloody men my life:
^{10} in whose hands is mischief, furthermore
their right hand with bribes is rife.

^{11} As for me, though, I will walk in mine integrity:
ransom me, and mercy show toward
me. ^{12} My foot doth stand on level ground: in the
congregations I will bless the LORD.

Psalm 27

· The Lord's my light and my deliverance; whom shall I fear?
The Lord's my life's redoubt; of whom shall I have dismay?
²When on me the wicked, yea, mine enemies and foes,
came to eat my flesh up, tripped and tumbled they.

³Though an army should encamp against me, my
heart shall not be fearful: though advance
should a war against me, confident will
I be even in this circumstance.

·⁴One thing have I desired of the Lord, that will I seek:
that in Jehovah's house I may tarry all of the
days of mine extent, to view the beauty of the Lord,
and to make within his temple inquiry.

⁵For in time of trouble he shall hide me in
his pavilion: in the secret space
of his tabernacle he shall hide me;
high upon a rock shall he me place.

·⁶And now above mine enemies around me shall my head
be lifted up: and sacrifices of clamoring
will I offer in his tabernacle; I will sing,
yea, unto Jehovah praises I will sing.

⁷Hear, O Lord, when with my voice I cry: and have
mercy on me, and to me reply.
⁸When thou saidest, Seek my face; to thee my
heart said, Seek thy face, O Lord, will I.

⁹Hide thy face not far from me; thy servant put
not away in wrath: the help of me
thou hast been; abandon not me, neither
leave me, my salvation's Deity.

¹⁰When my father and my mother me forsake,
then the Lord will take me. ¹¹Teach thou me,
Lord, thy way, and due to mine opponents,
lead me in a path of equity.

¹²Over to the will of mine opponents do
not deliver me: because on me
witnesses of falsehood are uprisen,
also such as breathe out cruelty.

¹³I would have fainted, were it not that I believed to see
Jehovah's goodness in the land of the animate.
¹⁴Wait upon Jehovah: be courageous, and thy heart
he shall strengthen: I say, on Jehovah wait.

Psalm 28

¹ Unto thee I'll cry, O Lord
my rock; to me remain not mum:
lest, if thou to me be silent, like
them that to the pit descend I should become.

²Hear the voice of mine entreaties,
when I cry aloud to thee,
when I lift my hands toward thine
oracle of sanctity.

³Draw me not away with the
ungodly, and with them who work
wickedness, the ones which speak to their
neighbors peace, but in their hearts doth mischief lurk.

⁴Give to them as to their deeds,
according to the wickedness
of their doings: give them after their
hands' endeavors; render to them their redress.

⁵For regard they not the works of
Yahweh, nor activity
of his hands, he shall destroy
them, and build them up shan't he.

⁶Blessed be the Lord, because the
voice of mine entreaties he
hath perceived. ⁷The Lord is the
fortitude and shield of me;

trust in him my heart did, and I
am assisted: therefore my
heart rejoiceth greatly; and
with my song will praise him I.

⁸Yahweh is their strength, he's his
anointed's saving strength, too. ⁹Thy
people save, and bless thy heritance:
feed them also, and forever lift them high.

Psalm 29

Ascribe to Yahweh, O ye sons of God,
ascribe to Yahweh weight and fortitude.
²Ascribe to Yahweh glory due his name;
to Yahweh bow in holy pulchritude.

³The voice of Yahweh on the waters is;
the God of glory roareth thund'rously;
upon the many waters Yahweh is.
⁴The voice of Yahweh is with potency;

the voice of Yahweh is with majesty.
⁵The voice of Yahweh breaketh cedar trees;
yea, Yahweh breaketh cedars Lebanese.
⁶To skip, too, like a calf he maketh these;

· like a son of oxen, Lebanon and Sirion.
⁷The voice of Yahweh doth the flames of fire split.
⁸The voice of Yahweh shaketh wilderness;
the wilderness of Kadesh — Yahweh shaketh it..

⁹The voice of Yahweh maketh female deer
to calve, and strippeth he the forests bare:
moreover in the temple of the Lord,
his glory ev'ry person doth declare.

¹⁰Upon the deluge Yahweh sitteth; yea,
as King shall Yahweh sit for timelessness.
¹¹Unto his people, strength will Yahweh give;
his people Yahweh with a peace will bless.

Psalm 30

¹ O L ORD, thee I'll extol; for thou hast lifted me,
and over me hast not allowed my foes to be
jubilant. ²O L ORD my God, I cried
unto thee, and thou hast healed me.

³From the sepulchre my soul
thou, O Y AHWEH, up hast brought:
thou hast let me live, that down
into the pit should go I not.

⁴Sing unto the L ORD, O ye
holy ones of his, profess
gratitude as well at the
remembrance of his holiness.

⁵Because his wrath endureth momentarily;
but in his favor there is life: though for a night
weeping may endure, at break of day
cometh exclamation of delight.

⁶And I, in my prosperity, said, Never shall
I totter. ⁷By thy favor thou, O L ORD, hast made
stand with strength my mountain: thou didst thy
countenance conceal; I was dismayed.

⁸I cried to thee, O L ORD; and supplication to
the L ORD I made. ⁹What profit in my blood is there,
when descend I to the pit? Shall praise
thee the dust? Shall it thy truth declare?

¹⁰L ORD, hear and show me mercy: be my helper, L ORD.
¹¹Thou hast transformed for me my mourning into dance:
thou hast put my sackcloth off, and thou
hast engirded me with jubilance;

¹²to the end that glory may
sing acclaim to thee, and be
silent not. O L ORD my God,
I'll give for ever thanks to thee.

Psalm 31

In thee, O Lord, I put my trust; let me
never be ashamed: deliver me
in thy righteousness. ²Incline thou thine
ear to me; me rescue speedily:

be thou my rock of strength, a fortified
house to save me. ³For my rock and fort
art thou; therefore for thy name's account,
thou shalt lead me, and shalt me escort.

⁴From net that privily they've laid for me
pull me: for thou art my potency.
⁵I commit my spirit to thy hand:
thou, Lord God of truth, hast ransomed me.

⁶I have hated them that honor lying vanities:
but in the Lord confide I. ⁷In thy love steadfast
I will gladden and rejoice: for mine affliction thou
hast beheld; in troubles, known my soul thou hast;

⁸and hast not shut me up into the hand
of the foe: thou hast positioned my
feet within a spacious room. ⁹On me,
Lord, have mercy, for in straits am I:

with vexation is consumed mine eye, indeed, my soul
and belly. ¹⁰For my life's exhausted with lament,
and my years with sighing: due to mine iniquity,
staggereth my strength, my bones are also spent.

¹¹To all mine enemies I was a scorn,
but among my neighbors specially,
and a fear to mine acquaintance: they
that without did see me fled from me.

¹²I'm out of mind, forgotten as a dead
man: I'm like a broken implement.
¹³For I've heard the defamation of
many: fear was circumambient:

while took together counsel they against
me, to take away my life they planned.
¹⁴But in thee I trusted, Lord: I said,
Thou: my God. ¹⁵My times are in thy hand;

deliver thou me from the hand of my
foes, and from my persecutors.[16] Make
thou thy face to on thy servant shine:
save me for thy lovingkindness' sake.

[17] Lord, let me not be shamed; for thee I've called:
let the wicked ones confuted be,
 and let them be silent in the grave.
[18] Let the lips of falsehood muted be;

· which in pride and scorn speak grievous things against the just.
[19] How great thy goodness is, which thou hast laid aside
for the ones that fear thee; which thou hast prepared for them
that, before the sons of men, in thee confide!

[20] Thou shalt conceal them from the pride of man
in thy face's covert: secretly
thou shalt keep them from the strife of tongues
in a booth.[21] Jehovah blessèd be:

· for his wondrous lovingkindness he hath showed me in
a city under siege.[22] For I had said in my
haste, I'm severed from before thine eyes: but heardest thou
mine entreaties' voice when cry to thee did I.

·[23] Love the Lord, his holy persons all: because the Lord
doth guard the faithful and the doer proud reward
plentifully.[24] Be ye of good courage, and your heart
he shall strengthen, all ye hopers in the Lord.

Psalm 32

- Blessed is the one whose trespass is forgiv'n,
whose sin is covered over. [2]Bless'd is the
man to whom the LORD imputeth not iniquity,
and in whose spirit is no falsity.

- [3]When remained I mum, my bones degraded through
my roaring all the day. [4]Because on me,
heavy was thy hand both day and night: my moisture's turned
into the summertime's aridity.   *Selah.*

- [5]I acknowledged unto thee my sin, and mine
iniquity I've hid not. I professed,
To the LORD I will admit to my transgressions; and
my sin's iniquity thou forgavest.   *Selah.*

- [6]For this cause shall ev'ry one that's godly pray
to thee in time when found thou mayest be:
in the inundations of abundant waters they
shall not attain to him assuredly.

[7]Thou my place of hiding art;
me thou shalt keep from sufferance;
encompass me about shalt thou with songs
of deliverance.   *Selah.*

[8]I will make thee circumspect
and I will teach thee in the course
which thou shalt go: I'll guide thee with mine eye.
[9]Be not as the horse,

neither as the mule, which have
no understanding; which must be
with bit and bridle held by mouth, lest come
near they unto thee.

- [10]To the wicked many griefs are: mercy, though,
shall ring the truster in the LORD about.
[11]Gladden in the LORD, and jubilate, ye righteous: and
in gladness all ye upright-hearted shout.

Psalm 33

In the L ord rejoice, ye righteous ones:
for praise is comely for the upright beings.
²With harp acclaim ye Yahweh: sing to him
with psaltery, a zither of ten strings.

³Sing to him an anthem new; adeptly play
with shout. ⁴For Yahweh's word is right; and all of his
works are done in truth. ⁵He loveth righteousness
and judgment: full the earth of Yahweh's goodness is.

⁶By the word of Yahweh were the heavens made;
and all their host by breath of his mouth. ⁷As a heap,
gathereth together he the waters of
the sea: in treasuries he layeth up the deep.

⁸All the earth shall fear the Lord: let all
indwellers of the world be afraid
of him. ⁹Because he spake, and into being
it came; commanded he, and fast it stayed.

¹⁰Yahweh rendereth the heathen's counsel nought:
the peoples' purposes he also doth restrain.
¹¹Standeth evermore the counsel of the Lord,
to generations all his heart's designs remain.

¹²Bless'd the nation is of which the Lord
is God; the people whom hath chosen he
for his inheritance. ¹³From heav'n the Lord
doth look; the sons of men he all doth see.

¹⁴From his place of habitation he
attendeth unto all the residents
of earth. ¹⁵He fashioneth their hearts alike;
he heedeth all of their accomplishments.

¹⁶There's no king who's saved by multitude of host:
a mighty man is not delivered by much strength.
¹⁷Treacherous for safety is a horse: and he
shall not deliver any by his massive strength.

¹⁸Lo, the eye of Yahweh is upon
his fearers, them that for his mercy wait;
¹⁹to snatch their soul away from death, and in
the famine to their lives perpetuate.

[20] Tarrieth our soul for YAHWEH: he's our help
and shield. [21] Because our heart shall joy in him, for we
in his holy name have trusted. [22] Let, O LORD,
thy mercy be upon us, as we hope in thee.

Psalm 34

¹ I will bless the LORD in seasons all:
in my mouth shall be his praise continually.
²In the LORD my soul shall make her boast:
hear thereof the humble shall, and joyful be.

³Magnify the LORD along with me,
and let us exalt his name in unity.
⁴Sought the LORD I, and he answered me,
and from all my terrors he delivered me.

⁵Unto him they looked, and lightened were:
and ashamed were not their countenances. ⁶Call
out did this poor man, and YAHWEH heard,
and he saved him out of his distresses all.

⁷YAHWEH's angel campeth round about
them that fear him, and them he delivereth.
⁸Taste and see ye that the LORD is good:
blessèd is the man that in him sheltereth.

⁹Fear the LORD, O ye his holy ones:
for to them that fear him there's no deficit.
¹⁰Youthful lions want and hunger: but
they that seek the LORD shall lack no benefit.

¹¹Come, ye children, hearken unto me:
I will teach the fear of YAHWEH unto you.
¹²Who's the man that wanteth life, and that
loveth many days, that goodness he may view?

¹³Keep thy tongue from evil, and
thy lips from speaking artifice.
¹⁴Depart from evil, and do good;
seek for peace, and follow after this.

¹⁵YAHWEH's eyes are on the righteous ones,
and his ears are open to their cry. ¹⁶The face
of the LORD's against the doers wrong,
to excise from earth their memorative trace.

¹⁷Cry the righteous, and the LORD doth hear,
and doth rescue them from all their spaces tight.
¹⁸YAHWEH's nigh to them of broken heart;
and he saveth those whose spirit is contrite.

¹⁹Many are the troubles of
the righteous, but from ev'ry one
the Lord doth snatch him. ²⁰Keepeth he
all his bones; of them is broken none.

²¹Evil shall dispatch the wicked: and
they that hate the righteous shall be desolate.
²²Yahweh ransometh his servants' soul:
and no truster in him shall be desolate.

Psalm 35

Lord, strive with them that strive with me:
fight against the ones that battle me.
^{2}Take ahold of shield and buckler, and
stand thou up in help of me.

^{3}And draw thou out the javelin,
also stop the way to counter my
persecutors: say unto my soul,
Thy deliverance am I.

^{4}Let them that seek to take my soul
be ashamed and rattled: let them be
backward turned and to confusion brought
that devise mine injury.

· ^{5}Let them be as chaff before the wind: let the
angel of Jehovah chase them, too.
^{6}Let their way be dark and slippery:
and the angel of Jehovah them pursue.

· ^{7}For without a cause they've hid their net for me
in a pit, which undeservedly
for my soul they've digged. ^{8}Upon him let
devastation come when unaware is he;

· and let catch himself his net that he hath hid:
let him fall to ruin in that pit.
^{9}And my soul shall in the Lord rejoice:
jubilant in his salvation shall be it.

· ^{10}All my bones shall say, Lord, who is like to thee,
which deliverest the poor from him
that's too strong for him, indeed, the poor
and the needy one from him that spoileth him?

^{11}Malicious witnesses arose;
things I knew not to my charge they laid.
^{12}Unto the bereavement of my soul,
bad for good they me repaid.

^{13}But as for me, when they were sick,
sackcloth was my clothing: I depressed
mine own soul with fasting; also my
prayer returned to mine own chest.

^{14}Behave myself did I as though
he had been my friend or brother: I
bowed disconsolately down, as one
that doth for his mother cry.

^{15}But in mine adversity rejoiced they, and
gathered they themselves together: yea,
gather did the abject ones against
me, and I knew not; they tore, and ceased not they:

^{16}with the mockers hypocritical in feasts,
with their teeth they gnashed on me. ^{17}Lord, how
long wilt look thou? Bring my soul from their
wastes; restore my darling from the lions thou.

^{18}In the congregation great I'll give thee thanks:
in the mighty people will I thee
praise. ^{19}Let not the ones that wrongfully
are mine enemies be joyful over me:

nor let them wink with eye that hate
me for nought. ^{20}For they do not express
peace: but craft they words of fraud against
them that in the land quiesce.

^{21}Yea, they opened wide their mouth against me, and
said, Aha, aha, our eye hath viewed.
^{22}Thou hast seen, Lord: keep thou silence not:
far, O Lord, from me do not thyself seclude.

^{23}Stir thyself, and to my judgment wake, to my
cause, my God and Master. ^{24}Judge thou me,
Lord my God, according unto thy
righteousness; and let them not rejoice o'er me.

^{25}Let them say not in their hearts, Aha, our wish!
Let them say not, Swallowed him have we.
^{26}Let them altogether be ashamed
and abashed that gladden at mine injury:

let them that boost themselves against
me be clothed with shame and with disgrace.
^{27}Let them shout for joy and jubilate,
that desire my righteous case:

· yea, let them say always, Let J‍ehovah be
magnified, which doth the peace desire
of his servant.[28] And my tongue shall speak
of thy justice and thy praise the day entire.

Psalm 36

Within my heart the trespass of the wicked
doth say: Before his eyes, there is of God no dread.
²For he in his own eyes himself doth adulate,
until his wickedness be found to merit hate.

³The sayings of his mouth are fraud and falsehood:
he hath desisted to be wise, and to do good.
⁴Upon his bed, he planneth mischief; standeth he
in way not good; he spurneth not malignancy.

⁵Lord, in the heavens, is thy lovingkindness;
and to the firmament doth reach thy faithfulness.
⁶Thy justice is like mountains great; a plumbless deep
thy judgments are: O Lord, thou man and beast dost keep.

⁷How excellent, God, is thy lovingkindness! Thus
in shadow of thy wings the sons of men commit their trust.

⁸They shall be satisfied abundantly off
the fatness of thy house; and thou shalt make them quaff
the river of thy delicacies. ⁹For with thee
the fount of life is: in thy light shall light we see.

¹⁰Prolong thy mercy to the people that thee know;
thy righteousness unto the upright ones in heart also.

¹¹Let not the foot of pride against me come, and
let not remove me the ungodly persons' hand.
¹²There fallen are the workers of iniquity:
they down are cast, and fit to rise they shall not be.

Psalm 37

· Be kindled not because of evildoers, nor
envious be thou of them that carry out
iniquity. ^{2}For they shall soon be cut
down like grass, and wither as the verdant sprout.

· ^{3}Confide in YAHWEH, and do good; so shalt thou dwell
in the land, and fed thou verily shalt be.
^{4}Delight thyself in YAHWEH also; and
the desires of thy heart shall give he thee.

· ^{5}Thy way commit unto the LORD; moreover in
him confide; and he shall cause it to ensue.
^{6}He also shall bring forth thy righteousness
as the light, thy judgment as the noonday, too.

· ^{7}In YAHWEH rest, and patiently await him: fret
not thyself by reason of the person who
doth prosper in his way, because of the
man who carrieth devices wicked through.

^{8}From anger cease, and wrath forsake:
do not ignite thyself as to
do any evil. ^{9}For cut off
shall be the ones that evil do:

but those that wait upon the LORD,
they shall inherit the terrain.
^{10}For yet a little while, and
the wicked one shall not remain:

· yea, diligently shalt consider thou his place,
and it shan't be. ^{11}Them, though, of humility
shall occupy the earth; and take delight
shall they in abundance of tranquility.

^{12}The wicked plotteth 'gainst the just,
and gnasheth on him with his teeth.
^{13}The Lord shall laugh at him because
that coming is his day he seeth.

·^{14}The wicked ones have drawn the sword, and bent their bow,
for to fell the low and poor, to slaughter those
of upright conversation. ^{15}Enter their
heart shall their own sword, and crushed shall be their bows.

^{16}The little of a righteous man is better than
the abundant wealth of many wicked. ^{17}For
the arms of the ungodly ones shall be
broken: but the righteous ones doth Yahweh shore.

^{18}The Lord doth know the days of the unblemished: and
their possession shall be for eternity.
^{19}They shall not be ashamed in evil time:
and in days of famine they shall sated be.

^{20}But perish shall the wicked, and
the foes of Yahweh as the bloom
of fields shall be: consume shall they;
away in smoke they shall consume.

^{21}The wicked borroweth, and he repayeth not:
but the righteous demonstrateth clemency,
and giveth. ^{22}For possess the earth shall those
bless'd of him; those cursed of him cut off shall be.

^{23}The footsteps of a godly man are ordered by
Yahweh: he delighteth also in his way.
^{24}Although he fall, he shan't be utterly
prostrated: because his hand the Lord doth stay.

^{25}I have been young, and now am old; yet I have not
seen the righteous one forsaken, neither his
descendants begging bread. ^{26}He's gracious all
day, and lendeth; and his seed a blessing is.

^{27}Depart from evil, and do good;
and dwell in perpetuity.
^{28}For Yahweh loveth judgment, and
abandoneth his saints not he;

for ever they are kept: but seed
of wicked ones cut off shall be.
^{29}The righteous shall possess the land,
and dwell therein eternally.

^{30}The just one's mouth doth wisdom speak;
of judgment, too, his tongue doth talk.
^{31}Within his heart is his God's law;
shall slide no footsteps of his walk.

³²The wicked watcheth for the just,
   and seeketh after him to kill.
³³The LORD won't leave him in his hand,
   nor when he's judged condemn him will.

³⁴Upon the LORD await, and keep
   his way, and lift thee up shall he
   to occupy the land: when off
   are cut the wicked, thou shalt see.

³⁵The wicked one have I beheld in power great,
   spreading also like a verdant native tree.
³⁶He passed away, though, and, lo, he was not:
   yea, I looked for him, but found he could not be.

³⁷Observe the perfect, and behold
   the upright: for the latter end
   of him is peace. ³⁸But utterly
   destroyed shall be them that offend:

   the wicked people's end shall be
   cut off. ³⁹But from the LORD is the
   salvation of the just, their strength
   in season of adversity.

⁴⁰And help them shall the LORD, and them
   deliver: from the wicked he
   shall them deliver, and them save,
   for they to him for refuge flee.

Psalm 38

^{1} JEHOVAH, in thy wrath rebuke me not:
nor in thy displeasure hot me reprimand.
^{2}For in me descend thine arrows, and
sore upon me doth descend thy hand.

^{3}Owing to thine anger, there's no
soundness in my skin;
in my bones there is no peace, by
reason of my sin.

^{4}For o'er my head are mine iniquities
gone: unduly heavy, as a heavy load,
are they for me. ^{5}On account of my
folly, stink my wounds, and they corrode.

^{6}Distorted am I; I am greatly bowed
down; in mourning all the day I go around.
^{7}For my loins are filled with burning: and
in my flesh not any part is sound.

^{8}I'm feeble and severely broken: by
reason of the tumult of my heart I've roared.
^{9}My desire is all before thee; and
hid from thee is not my groaning, Lord.

^{10}My heart pulsateth, faileth me my strength:
and the light, too, of mine eyes from me is gone.
^{11}From my sore, my lovers and my friends
stand aloof; my kinsmen stand withdrawn.

^{12}The ones that seek to take my life, too, lay
snares for me: and they that seek mine evil say
things injurious, moreover they
meditate deceptions all the day.

^{13}But as one deaf, I heard not; and I was
as a mute that openeth his mouth not wide.
^{14}Thus I was as one that heareth not,
who hath in his mouth no words to chide.

^{15}Because in thee, O LORD, I hope: thou wilt
hear, O Lord my God. ^{16}For otherwise, said I,
over me they should rejoice: when my
foot doth slip, on me they magnify.

[17] For I am ready to collapse, and my
sorrow is continually in front of me.
[18] For I'll tell of mine iniquity;
for my sin, regretful will I be.

[19] But mine enemies are lively;
they're in number great:
also they are multiplied that
wrongfully me hate.

[20] Also they that render bad in
place of good are mine
adversaries; for I follow
after what is fine.

[21] Leave me not, O LORD: my God, be
not thou far from me.
[22] Hasten thou, O Lord, to help me,
my delivery.

Psalm 39

[1] I will guard my ways, I said, that I
sin not with my tongue: my mouth I will
keep with bridle, while the wicked one
is before me. [2] I was dumb and still,

silence I preserved, from even good;
and my pain was roiled. [3] My heart did bake
in mine inward part, the fire burned
as I mused: then with my tongue I spake,

[4] JEHOVAH, make me know mine end,
and what the length of my
days is; so that I may
know how frail am I.

[5] Lo, a handbreadth thou hast made my days;
and mine age as nought in front of thee:
surely ev'ry person at his best
state is altogether vanity.　　　　*Selah.*

[6] Surely in an image walketh man:
surely they are clamorous in vain:
heapeth up he riches, knoweth he
not, though, who shall come to them obtain.

[7] And now, Lord, what wait I for? My hope
is in thee. [8] Deliver thou me from
all of my transgressions: make thou me
not the fool's derision. [9] I was dumb,

I opened not my mouth; because
thou didst. [10] From me retract
thou thy stroke: I'm finished
by thy hand's impact.

[11] When thou with rebukes correctest man
for misconduct, what to him is dear
makest thou to vanish like a moth:
surely ev'ry man is vapor mere.　　　　*Selah.*

[12] Hear my prayer, LORD; hearken to my cry;
hold thy peace not when my teardrops fall:
for with thee I am a stranger, an
alien, as were my fathers all.

[13] Remove thy gaze from me, that I
may smile again, before
go I hence, and there be
not me anymore.

Psalm 40

· Patiently I waited for J‍ehovah; and
unto me inclined he, and my cry he heard.
²And he brought me up out of a rackety
cistern, from the miry clay, my feet then he
positioned on a rock; my goings he secured.

· ³In my mouth an anthem new hath put he, praise
to our God: a multitude shall see, and fear,
and shall hope upon the L‍ord. ⁴He's blessèd who
doth appoint the L‍ord his trust and turn not to
the insolent, nor such as unto falsehood veer.

· ⁵Many, L‍ord my God, are thine amazing works
thou hast done, as well thy thoughts which are toward us:
they cannot be reckoned to thee in array:
if I were to give account then I would say
of them, they are innumerably numerous.

· ⁶Sacrifice and offering thou didst not take
pleasure in; the ears of me hast thou unclosed:
thou hast not required burnt offering and sin
offering. ⁷Then I declared, Lo, come I: in
the volume of the book it is of me composed,

· ⁸I delight to do thy will, my God: indeed,
in my heart thy law is. ⁹Tidings glad I've brought —
righteousness — into the great assembly: lo,
I have not refrained my lips, L‍ord, thou dost know.
¹⁰Within my heart thy righteousness have hid I not;

declared have I thy faithfulness
and deliverance:
I've not concealed thy kindness and thy truth
from the many congregants.

¹¹Withhold thy tender mercies not
thou, O L‍ord, from me:
allow thy lovingkindness and thy truth
to preserve me constantly.

¹²For innumerable evils have about
me encompassed: hold upon myself have took
mine iniquities, so that to look above
I'm not able; they are more than bristles of
my head: my heart hath consequently me forsook.

¹³Pleased be, O JEHOVAH, to deliver me:
O JEHOVAH, hasten to mine aid. ¹⁴Let be
shamed and mortified together them that track
down my soul to snatch it; let be driven back
and put to shame them that desire mine injury.

¹⁵Let the ones be desolate as a reward
of their shame that say, Aha, aha, to me.
¹⁶All that seek thee let rejoice and be elate
in thee: may those loving thy salvation state
continually, May magnified JEHOVAH be.

¹⁷I'm poor and needy; yet the Lord
of me taketh thought:
thou art my help and my deliverer;
O my God, delay thou not.

Psalm 41

· Bless'd is he that thinketh of the one in poverty:
save him will the LORD in day of devilry.

² The LORD will guard him, and him he will keep alive;
and he shall be bless'd upon the land:
also thou wilt not deliver him
into his opponents' hand.

·³ On the bed of languishing, the LORD him strengthen will:
all his bed wilt overturn thou in his ill.

⁴ I said, O LORD, to me be gracious: heal my soul;
for I've sinned against thee. ⁵ Evil mine
enemies express of me, When shall
die he, and his name decline?

⁶ And if he come to see me, vanity then he
speaketh: gathereth iniquity
to itself his heart; when he abroad
goeth forth, proclaimeth he.

·⁷ Unified against me whisper all them that me hate:
they against me evil for me formulate.

·⁸ Cleaveth fast to him, say they, an evil malady:
now then that he lieth, rise no more shall he.

·⁹ Yea, my man of peace, in whom I trusted, which of my
bread did eat, hath raised his heel against me high.

·¹⁰ But incline thou unto me with graciousness, O LORD,
raise me up, too, so that them I may reward.

·¹¹ By this I perceive that thou dost take delight in me,
for my hater doth not triumph over me.

·¹² As for me, thou holdest me in mine integrity,
and before thy face forever settest me.

·¹³ From the eon and unto the eon blessèd be
YAHWEH God of Israel. So be, and so be.

Book II

Psalm 42

· As the hart doth pant for water brooks,
so doth pant my soul, O God, for thee.
²Thirst for God, the living God, doth my
soul: when shall I come and God's face see?

³Day and night my tears have been
meat to me, while blare
they continually unto
me: Thy God is where?

⁴When remember I these things,
pour then out I my
soul in me: for with the throng,
overpassed had I,

went with them I to God's house,
with the voice of glee
and of praise, a throng that kept
day of sanctity.

· ⁵Why art thou cast down, my soul? And why
roarest thou within me? Hope in God:
for yet unto him, for saving acts
of his countenance, shall give I laud.

· ⁶O my God, in me my soul is cast
down: remember thee I therefore will
from the land of Jordan, and of the
peaks of Hermon, from Mizar the hill.

⁷At the thunder of thy spouts,
deep to deep doth call:
over me are gone thy waves
and thy billows all.

· ⁸Yet JEHOVAH will command in the
day his lovingkindness, and his ayre
shall be with me in the nighttime, and
to my life's Divinity my prayer.

· ⁹Unto God my shielder will I
question, Why hast thou forgotten me?
Why do go I mourning on account
of oppression of the enemy?

¹⁰With a sword into my bones,
taunt me do my foes
with the question, Where's thy God?,
that they daily pose.

¹¹Why art thou cast down, my soul? And why
roarest thou within me? Hope in God:
for yet I shall praise him, who's the health
of my countenance, as well my God.

Psalm 43

Judge me, God, and plead thou my cause
against a nation merciless:
O deliver me from the
man of fraud and wickedness.

[2] For thou art the God of my strength:
why castest thou me off? Why go
I in mourning on account
of oppression of the foe?

[3] Send thou out thy light and thy truth:
let them direct me; let them goad
me unto thy holy hill,
and the tents of thine abode.

[4] Then unto the altar of God
will I proceed, to God the glee
of my joy: yea, God my God,
on the harp will praise I thee.

[5] Why art thou cast down, my soul? And why
roarest thou within me? Hope in God:
for yet I shall praise him, who's the health
of my countenance, as well my God.

Psalm 44

We've heard with our own ears, God, our
fathers have us told,
of the work thou didst in their
days, in times of old.

²Thou oustedst nations with thy hand,
plantedst them as well;
thou didst plague the people, and
thou didst them expel.

³Because by their own sword did not
they the land obtain,
neither did for them their own
arm salvation gain:

· but 'twas thy right hand, and thine arm,
and luster of thy countenance,
for them thou didst favor. ⁴Thou my King, O God,
art: for Jacob, order thou deliverance.

· ⁵Through thee will push we down our foes,
and through thy name will trample we
them that rise against us. ⁶For I will not trust
in my bow; my sword shall not deliver me.

· ⁷But from our enemies thou hast
us saved, and thou hast put to shame
them that hated us. ⁸In God we all the day
boast, and for eternity we'll praise thy name.
Selah.

· ⁹But thou hast spurned us, and us put
to shame; and goest not abroad
with our hosts. ¹⁰Thou makest us turn back from foe:
also they which hate us for themselves maraud.

· ¹¹Us thou hast made like sheep for meat;
and in the nations hast us strewed.
¹²Sellest thou for nought thy people, and by their
price dost not increase thy riches' magnitude.

¹³Unto our neighbors a reproach
renderest thou us,
a derision and a scorn
to them circling us.

^{14}Among the infidels, a saw
   renderest thou us,
   and a shaking of the head
   mid the populace.

^{15}Mine ignominy is before
   me continually,
   also the disgrace of my
   face hath covered me,

^{16}because the voice of him that doth
   blaspheme and berate;
   on account of foe and him
   that doth vindicate.

^{17}On us is all this come; yet we've
   not forgotten thee,
   neither falsely dealt in thy
   covenant have we.

^{18}Our heart's not backward turned, nor from
   thy way have strayed our steps;^{19}though sore
   broken us hast thou in place of dragons; and
   with the shade of death, us thou hast covered o'er.

^{20}If we've forgotten our God's name,
   or spread apart our hands have we
   to a foreign god;^{21}shall God not search this out?
   For the secrets of the heart perceiveth he.

^{22}Indeed, for thine account are killed
   we all the day; as sheep to slay
   we are counted.^{23}Waken, Lord, why sleepest thou?
   Rise up, cast us not for evermore away.

^{24}Why dost conceal thou thy face,
   and forget our woe
   and distress?^{25}For to the dust,
   bowed our soul is low:

   our belly cleaveth to the earth.
^{26}For our succour mount,
   and redeem thou us on thy
   kindnesses' account.

Psalm 45

With a matter good doth gush my heart:
my composition I recite
to the king: my tongue's the pen of a
person who is quick to write.

·²Thou art fairer than the sons of men: into
thy lips is favor poured: thus God hath thee
bless'd for ever. ³Gird thy sword on thigh, O most
mighty, with thy glory and thy majesty.

⁴And advance thou in thy splendor. Ride
because of truth and meekness and
righteousness; moreover, teach thee things
terrible shall thy right hand.

·⁵In the heart of haters of the king are sharp
thine arrows; fall the people under thee.
⁶God, thy throne is ever and forever: thy
kingdom's sceptre is a rod of equity.

⁷Righteousness thou lovest; wickedness
thou hatest: God, thy God, hath thee
thus anointed with the oil of
joy above thy company.

⁸Myrrh, and aloes, cassia as well,
to all thy garments give their scents;
from the palaces of ivory,
cheered thee have stringed instruments.

⁹Royal daughters were among thy dear:
the queen, in pure gold of Ophir,
stood upon thy right hand. ¹⁰See and hear,
daughter, and incline thine ear;

and forget thou thine own people, and
thy father's house; ¹¹the king shall so
much desire thy beauty: for he's thy
Lord; so bow unto him low.

·¹²Also Tyre's daughter shall be there with gift;
the rich among the people shall request
thy regard. ¹³The daughter of the king is all
glorious within: of woven gold's her vest.

¹⁴In attire of needlework, unto
the king shall be conducted she:
her companions, virgins trailing her,
shall be carried unto thee.

¹⁵Brought with joy and gladness shall be they: they'll come
into the palace of the potentate.
¹⁶In thy fathers' stead shall be thy sons, whom in
all the earth as princes mayest thou instate.

¹⁷I will make thy name to be recalled
in generations all: therefore
shall the people give to thee acclaim
ever and for evermore.

Psalm 46

God's our refuge and our potency:
a very present help in adversity.

²Therefore we won't be afraid, though earth be taken out,
and though into the heart of oceans slide
the mountains; ³though its waters clamor and ferment,
though undulate the mountains with its pride.   *Selah.*

⁴There exists a river, channels of the which shall make
rejoice the town of God, the holy spot
of tabernacles of the Highest. ⁵God is in
the midst of her, and moved shall she be not:

God shall help her at the break of dawn. ⁶The heathen raged,
the kingdoms slipped: his voice projected he,
the earth did melt. ⁷The Lord of armies is with us;
the God of Jacob's our security.   *Selah.*

⁸Come, behold the works of Yahweh ye,
what desolations made in the earth hath he.

⁹To the world's limit, he doth make
hostilities to cease; the bow he doth break,

and the spear in sunder he doth cut;
he burneth in the fire the chariot.

¹⁰Rest, and know that I am God: exalted will I be
among the heathen, in the earth will I
exalted be. ¹¹The Lord of armies is with us;
the God of Jacob is our tower high.   *Selah.*

Psalm 47

¹ O clap your hands, ye people all; unto
God with cry of joy vociferate.
²For terrible's the LORD supreme;
he's over all the earth a Monarch great.

³Subdue shall he the people under us,
and beneath our feet the nations. ⁴He
shall choose our heritage for us,
of Jacob, whom he loved, the majesty.
Selah.
⁵God is gone up with a shout,
JEHOVAH with the sound of trumpet. ⁶Sing
praises unto God, sing praises:
to our King sing praises, praises sing.

⁷For God's the King of the entire earth:
with an understanding, psalms intone.
⁸God reigneth o'er the heathen: God
doth sit upon his holiness' throne.

⁹The princes of the peoples are converged
as the people of the Deity
of Abraham: for shields of earth
belong to God: exalted much is he.

Psalm 48

Great's the LORD, and in the city of our
God he is to be
greatly praised, upon the mount
of his sanctity.

²Beautiful for situation, it
is the joy of the entire land:
mountain Zion, on the sides of the
north, the city of the Monarch grand.

³God is known within her palaces
for a refuge. ⁴For assembled, lo,
were the kings, together passed they by.
⁵Saw it they, thus marveled they also;

they were troubled, hasted they away.
⁶Fear possessed them there, indeed travail,
as a woman giving birth. ⁷The ships
of Tarshish thou breakest with east gale.

⁸In the city of the LORD of hosts,
just as we have heard, so seen have we,
in the city of our God: God will
stablish it unto eternity.   *Selah.*

⁹Of thy lovingkindness we have thought
in the middle of thy temple, God.
¹⁰God, according to thy name, so is
to the limits of the earth thy laud:

thy right hand is full of justice. ¹¹Let
mountain Zion joy, let be elate
Judah's daughters, on account of thy
judgments. ¹²Zion circumnavigate,

and proceed around her: number its
towers. ¹³Study ye her bulwarks well,
contemplate her palaces; that to
later generations ye may tell.

¹⁴For this God's our God forevermore and
to eternity:
even unto death he will
our conductor be.

Psalm 49

Hear this, all ye people; give
ear, ye persons all that bide
in the world: ²both low and high,
rich and poor ones, unified.

·³My mouth shall speak of wisdom; and my heart's
musing shall of understanding be.
⁴I will to a proverb turn mine ear
and my riddle open on the psaltery.

⁵Wherefore should I be afraid
in the days of devilry,
when iniquity of my
heels about shall compass me?

·⁶Of them that trust upon their wealth, and in
vastness of their riches speak with pride,
⁷no one can redeem his brother, nor
can for him a ransom unto God provide:

⁸(for the ransom of their soul's
precious, and for ever it
ceaseth:)⁹that for ever he
should have life, not see the pit.

¹⁰For he seeth that sages die,
so the daft and brutish kind
perish, and that they unto
others leave their wealth behind.

·¹¹Their inward thought is that their houses shall
evermore continue, and to all
generations their pavilions of
dwelling; after their own names their lands they call.

·¹²But though in honor, man abideth not:
like unto the beasts that cease is he.
¹³This their way is foolishness for them:
yet approve their sayings their posterity.   *Selah.*

¹⁴In the grave they're laid like sheep;
death shall feed upon them; and
over them the upright shall
in the morning have command;

· and in the underworld, far from their
 dwelling, shall their beauty atrophy.
¹⁵But redeem my soul will God from the
 power of the grave: for he shall take in me.   *Selah.*

¹⁶Fear thou not when one's enriched,
 when the glory should increase
 of his house;¹⁷ for he shall take
 nought away in his decease:

follow him below shan't his
 glory.¹⁸ Though his soul he bless'd
 while he lived: and thee they'll praise,
 when for thee thou well doest.

·¹⁹Unto his fathers' generation he'll
 go; not ever see the light shall they.
²⁰Man that is in honor, and doth not
 understand, is like the beasts that pass away.

Psalm 50

Spoken hath the mighty God, the Lord,
and the earth he hath addressed
from the sun's ascension in the east
to its setting in the west.

^{2}Out of Zion, the perfection of
beauty, God hath shined forth. ^{3}Our
God shall come, and shall not silence keep:
fire before him shall devour,

and about him very stormy it
shall be. ^{4}To the heavens he
from above shall call, and to the earth,
that may judge his people he.

^{5}Gather ye my saints together unto me;
those who've made a covenant with me
by sacrifice. ^{6}The heavens also shall declare
his righteousness: for God, the judge is he. *Selah.*

^{7}Hearken, O my people, and I will
speak; against thee testify
will I, furthermore. O Israel:
God, thy God indeed, am I.

^{8}For thy sacrifices I'll reprove thee not;
thy burnt off'rings are in front of me
continually. ^{9}I will take no bullock from
thy house, and neither from thy folds goats-he.

^{10}For to me is each forestial beast;
on a thousand hills the kine.
^{11}Know I all the fowls of mountains: and
wild beasts of field are mine.

^{12}If I hungered, I would tell thee not:
for the world is mine, its fill
also. ^{13}Will I eat the flesh of bulls,
or the blood of he-goats swill?

^{14}Offer unto God a sacrifice of praise;
pay thy vows unto the One Most High:
^{15}and call upon me in the day of trouble: I
will free thee, and thou shalt me glorify.

¹⁶·To the wicked, though, God saith, What right hast thou
to declare my laws or take across
thy mouth my covenant?¹⁷For hatest thou reproof,
my words thou also dost behind thee toss.

¹⁸·When a thief thou sawest, thou consentedst with
him then, and hast taken part among
adulterers.¹⁹To evil givest thou thy mouth,
and formulate deception doth thy tongue.

²⁰·Thou dost sit and speak against thy brother; yea,
slanderest thou thine own mother's son.
²¹These things hast done thou, and yet silence I maintained;
thou thoughtest that I as thyself was one:

· but I will reprove thee, and in order set
them before thine eyes.²²Consider, ye
of God forgetful, this now lest in pieces you
I tear, and none there to deliver be.

²³Whosoever offereth acclaim
honoreth me: and display
God's deliverance will I to him
that arrangeth right his way.

Psalm 51

God, according to thy lovingkindness have
thou upon me clemency: annul
my transgressions in accord with the
greatness of thy graces merciful.

²Wash me throughly from mine iniquity;
purify me from my sin, too. ³For
I acknowledge my transgressions: my
sin's before me also evermore.

⁴I have sinned against thee, thee alone, and this
evil I've committed in thy view:
so that thou art justified when thou
speakest, blameless when thou judgest, too.

⁵Consider, I was shapen in iniquity;
and in sin my mother did conceive me. ⁶Lo,
thou desirest truth in inward parts: and in
the hidden part me thou shalt make to wisdom know.

⁷Purge thou me with hyssop, and I shall be clean:
wash me, and more white than snow I'll be.
⁸Make me hear delight and gladness; let
bones which thou hast broken leap with glee.

⁹From my sins thy countenance conceal; all
mine iniquities abolish, too.
¹⁰God, create in me a spotless heart;
and in me a spirit right renew.

¹¹From thy presence cast me not away; and take
thou thy holy spirit not from me.
¹²Thy salvation's joy to me restore;
and uphold me with thy spirit free.

¹³I'll teach transgressors then thy ways; and sinners shall
be converted unto thee. ¹⁴Deliver me,
God, from blood, thou God of my salvation: and
my tongue shall sing aloud of righteousness of thee.

¹⁵Open thou my lips, O Lord; my mouth then shall
tell thy praise. ¹⁶For thou dost not desire
sacrifice; else would I give it: thou
favorest not off'ring burnt by fire.

[17] God's sacrifices are a broken spirit; a
broken and a contrite heart wilt not contemn
thou, O God. [18] Do good in thy benevolence
to Zion: build the walls about Jerusalem.

[19] Then shalt thou be pleased with sacrifices of
righteousness, with the burnt offering
and the whole burnt offering: then shall
they upon thine altar bullocks bring.

Psalm 52

· Why dost thou in mischief boast thyself, O man of strength?
God's benevolence doth last the day's entire length.

²Thy tongue deviseth mischiefs; like a sharp
razor, laboring deceitfully.
³Thou lovest evil more than good; and more
than speaking righteousness, mendacity.　　　　　*Selah.*

·⁴All devouring words thou lovest, tongue of treachery.
⁵God shall thereupon destroy thee for eternity,

· he shall take thee up and pluck thee from thy place to dwell;
from the land of living beings, he'll root thee out as well.
　　　　　　　　　　　　　　　　　　Selah.
·⁶And the righteous ones shall see, and fear, and at him mock:
⁷This, consider, is the man that made not God his rock;

· but on the abundance of his riches he relied,
and in his cupidity himself he fortified.

·⁸But within God's house I'm like a verdant olive tree:
in God's mercy trust I always and eternally.

·⁹Thee I'll ever praise, for thou hast done it: and I'll bide
on thy name; for it is good before thy sanctified.

Psalm 53

In his heart the fool hath said, There is no God.
They're corrupt, and they have done
odious iniquity:
there that doeth good is none.

²God from heaven looked upon the sons of men,
to discover if there be
one that understood, that did
after God make inquiry.

³Ev'ry one of them is gone away: they are
altogether come to rot;
there is none that doeth good:
even one, no, there is not.

⁴Have no knowledge workers of iniquity?
Persons who devour my
people as they gobble bread:
unto God they do not cry.

⁵There were they in great alarm,
where was no alarm: because diffused
hath God his bones who doth encamp against thee:
thou hast them disgraced, for them hath God refused.

⁶Oh that the salvation of
Israel were out of Zion come!
When God doth turn the fortunes of his people,
Jacob shall be glad, and Israel gleesome.

Psalm 54

Save me by thy name, O God;
judge me by thy strength, too. ²Hear,
God, my prayer; unto my mouth's
sayings give thou ear.

³For against me strangers have
risen; tyrants, too, have sought
out my soul: and they have set
God before them not.   *Selah.*

⁴Lo, my help is God: with my
soul's upholders is the Lord.
⁵Evil shall he unto mine
enemies reward:

in thy truth destroy them. ⁶I'll
sacrifice of mine accord
unto thee: I'll praise thy name
for it's good, O LORD.

⁷For he hath delivered me
out of all adversities:
and mine eye hath seen his wish
on mine enemies.

Psalm 55

· Give ear unto my prayer, O God; and hide
 thyself from mine entreaty not.
 ²Attend to me, and answer me: I mourn
 in my complaint, and moan, distraught;

·³by reason of the adversary's voice
 and wicked one's oppression: for
 upon me they project iniquity,
 and they in anger me abhor.

·⁴My heart is sorely pained in me: and dreads
 of death are fallen down on me.
 ⁵Upon me fear and quivering are come,
 and shuddering hath covered me.

·⁶I said then, Oh that I had pinions like
 a dove! For then I'd fly away,
 and be at rest.⁷Lo, I would wander far,
 and in the wilderness would stay.   *Selah.*

·⁸From windy storm and tempest hasten my
 escape would I.⁹Destroy, O Lord,
 divide their tongues: for in the city I
 have witnessed cruelty and discord.

¹⁰Day and night upon the walls thereof,
 they about it go:
 within the midst of it as well
 are wickedness and woe.

·¹¹Within its midst is wickedness: deceit
 and guile depart not from her square.
 ¹²For it is not an enemy that me
 reproacheth; then it I could bear:

 neither was it he that hated me
 that did magnify
 himself against me; then have hid
 myself from him would I:

·¹³but it was thou, a man mine equal, my
 companion and acquaintance.¹⁴We
 together sweetened counsel, to the house
 of God we walked in company.

[15] Death shall seize upon them, they shall go
down alive to hell:
for wickedness among them is
within the place they dwell.

· [16] As for myself, though, I will call on God;
the LORD shall then deliver me.
[17] I'll pray in eve and morn, at noon as well,
and roar: and hear my voice shall he.

· [18] In peace my soul hath he delivered from
the war against me: for untold
were with me. [19] God shall hear, and them afflict,
yea he that doth abide of old.   *Selah.*

· Because they have no changes and no fear
of God. [20] Against the ones that be
at peace with him hath put he forth his hands:
his covenant hath broken he.

[21] Smoother was his mouth than butter, but
battle was upon
his heart; his words: more soft than oil,
yet they were sabers drawn.

[22] Cast upon the LORD thy burden, and
he shall nourish thee:
forever he shall not allow
the just to shaken be.

· [23] But thou, O God, shalt bring them down into
the pit of ruin: bloodthirsty
and underhanded men shan't live out half
their days; but I will trust in thee.

Psalm 56

God, to me be merciful: for man would swallow me
up; he fighting all the day oppresseth me.

^{2}All the day mine enemies would swallow up:
for many be the ones that loftily
battle me. ^{3}What time I am afraid,
confide will I in thee.

^{4}In God (I will praise his word), in God have put I my
trust; what flesh can do to me will fear not I.

^{5}Ev'ry day they wrest my words: against me all
their thoughts for evil are. ^{6}They congregate,
they conceal themselves, they mark my steps,
when for my soul they wait.

^{7}Shall they by iniquity deliverance acquire?
Cast, O God, thou down the people in thine ire.

^{8}Thou dost numerate my wand'rings: put my tears
into thy bottle: are they not in thy
book? ^{9}Then to the rear my foes shall turn
when unto thee I cry,

This I know: that God's for me. ^{10}In God (acclaim the word
will I), in JEHOVAH (I will praise the word),

^{11}I have put my trust in God: I will not be
afraid of that which man can do to me.
^{12}God, upon me are thy vows: I'll pay
thanksgivings unto thee.

^{13}For thou hast delivered from decease my soul:
from falling wilt thou not deliver my
feet, that walk before the face of God
in light of life may I?

Psalm 57

- Be merciful to me, O God, be merciful
  to me: because my soul doth put her trust in thee:
  indeed, I'll make my refuge in the shadow of
  thy wings, till overpast these devastations be.

² I will cry to God supreme; to God
  that for me performeth all things. ³ He
  shall send from heaven, and he shall me save.
  Reproacheth he him that would swallow me.   *Selah.*

- Send forth his mercy and his truth shall God. ⁴ My soul's
  in midst of lions: and I even lie among
  the persons set on fire, the sons of men, whose teeth
  are spears and arrows, and a saber sharp their tongue.

- ⁵ Above the heavens be exalted thou, O God;
  let over all the earth thy glory be. ⁶ They've spread
  a net out for my steps; my soul is bowed: they've digged
  a pit before me, in its midst they've plummeted.   *Selah.*

- ⁷ My heart is steadfast, God, my heart is steadfast: I
  will sing and give acclaim. ⁸ Awaken up, my soul;
  awaken, psaltery and harp: I'll early wake.
  ⁹ O Lord, among the people I will thee extol:

- To thee among the nations, psalms will I intone.
  ¹⁰ For great unto the heavens is thy mercy, and
  thy truth unto the clouds. ¹¹ Be raised, O God, above
  the heavens and thy glory over all the land.

Psalm 58

· Do truly speak ye righteousness, O silent ones?
Ye sons of men, do ye uprightly vindicate?
²Indeed, in heart ye work injustice; in the earth
the cruel doings of your hands ye contemplate.

· ³The wicked are estranged from womb: declaring lies,
as soon as they from belly come they go astray.
⁴Their poison's like the poison of a serpent: like
the adder deaf that stoppeth up her ear are they;

⁵which will hearken not unto the voice
of charmers, charming skillfully.
⁶Break their teeth, God, in their mouth: LORD, break
the youthful lions's great teeth free.

⁷Let them melt away as waters which
continually run: when he
bendeth bow to shoot his arrows, as
though cut in pieces let them be.

⁸As a snail which melteth into slime,
of them let vanish ev'ry one:
like a woman's stillborn baby, that
they never may behold the sun.

· ⁹Before your pots can feel the thorns, them he shall take
away as with a whirlwind, living and in heat.
¹⁰The righteous shall rejoice when seeth he vengeance: in
the blood of the ungodly he shall wash his feet.

¹¹Thereupon a man shall say, there is
a compensation verily
for the righteous: verily a God
that judgeth in the earth is he.

Psalm 59

· Deliver thou me from mine enemies,
   my God: from them that rise against me, me defend.
² From the workers of iniquity
   deliver me, and save me from the bloody men.

· ³ For, lo, they lie in ambush for my soul:
   assembled in attack against me are the strong;
   not for my transgression or my sin,
   O Lord. ⁴ They run and set themselves without my wrong:

· awake to help me, and behold. ⁵ And thou,
   Lord God of hosts, the God of Israel, awake
   to attend to nations all: on all
   the treacherous in wickedness no mercy take.   *Selah.*

· ⁶ At evening they return: they snarl like
   a dog, and circumnavigate the city they.
   ⁷ Witness that they belch out with their mouth:
   between their lips are swords: for who doth hear, they say?

⁸ But thou, O Lord, shalt laugh at them;
   thou shalt deride the heathen all.
⁹ By his power will I wait on thee: for
   God is mine asylum tall.

¹⁰ My mercy's God shall meet me: God,
   upon mine enemies, shall let
   me behold my longing. ¹¹ Slay them not, or
   else my people shall forget:

· disperse them by thy pow'r; and down them, Lord
   our shield. ¹² For sin within their mouth and words of their
   lips, let them be taken in their pride:
   and for the cursing and the lies that they declare.

¹³ Consume thou them in wrath, consume,
   that they may be no longer: and
   let them know that God in Jacob ruleth
   to the limits of the land.   *Selah.*

¹⁴ And in the eve let them return;
   and let them like a canine growl,
   and proceed around the city. ¹⁵ Let them
   up and down for victuals prowl,

and grudge if they're not satisfied.
¹⁶But of thy power I will sing;
also of thy lovingkindness will I
in the morning loudly sing:

· for thou hast been my lofty stronghold and
a refuge in the day of mine adversity.
¹⁷Unto thee, my strength, I'll sing: for God
is my defense, the God of my benignity.

Psalm 60

Thou, O God, hast cast us off, thou hast
scattered us abroad, thou hast been cross;
O again restore us. ²Thou hast made the earth to quake;
thou hast broken it: repair its cracks; for it doth toss.

³Thou hast showed thy people grievous things:
wine of drunken reeling thou hast made
us to drink. ⁴A banner hast thou given unto thy
fearers, that it may be, on account of truth, displayed.
                                                                Selah.
⁵That thy loved may be delivered; save
with thy right hand; hear me furthermore.
⁶God hath spoken in his holiness; I will rejoice,
Shechem I'll divide, I'll measure Succoth's valley floor.

⁷Gilead is mine, and mine
is Manasseh; also the
helmet of my head is Ephraim;
Judah giveth my decree;

⁸Moab is my washpot; fling
over Edom will I my
shoe: Philistia, because of me
make thou a triumphant cry.

⁹Who into the city strong will bring
me? Who into Edom will me lead?
¹⁰Will it not be thou, O God, thou who hadst cast us off?
And, O God, who with our armies didst not forth proceed?

¹¹Give us help from trouble: for
help of man is vanity.
¹²Valiantly through God shall do we: for
trample down our foes shall he.

Psalm 61

Hear my cry, O God; attend to my
prayer. [2] From the extremity of earth I'll cry
unto thee at time my heart is overwhelmed:
lead me to the rock that's loftier than I.

[3] For a shelter thou hast been for me,
from the enemy a tower strong. [4] Abide
will I in thy tabernacle evermore:
in the covert of thy wings will I confide. *Selah.*

[5] For thou, God, hast heard my vows: thou hast
given me the heritage of those with fear
of thy name. [6] Thou wilt prolong the life of the
king: to generations shall extend his years.

[7] He shall sit before God evermore:
O prepare thou steadfast love and truth, which may
guard him. [8] So I'll sing acclaim unto thy name
always, that I may perform my vows each day.

Psalm 62

· Verily my soul doth wait on God: from him
cometh my salvation. ²Only he
is my rock and my salvation; he is my
fortress; greatly moved I shall not be.

³How long will ye rush upon
a man? Ye all shall slaughtered be:
as a bowing wall, and as
a fence unstable shall be ye.

⁴Take they counsel only to
expel him from his dignity:
lies they relish: with their mouth
they bless, but curse they inwardly.   *Selah.*

· ⁵O my soul, on God alone await; for from
him's mine expectation. ⁶Only he
is my rock and my salvation: he is my
lofty fortress; moved I shall not be.

· ⁷My salvation and my glory is in God:
my strong rock, my refuge, is in God.
⁸Trust in him in seasons all; before him, ye
people, pour your heart; our shelter's God.   *Selah.*

· ⁹Surely men of low degree are vanity,
and a lie are men of high degree:
to be weighed upon the balances, they are
lighter all at once than vanity.

¹⁰Trust not in oppression, and
become not vain in robbery:
if increase should riches, then
upon them set your heart not ye.

· ¹¹God hath spoken once; I twice have heard this; that
pow'r belongeth unto God. ¹²With thee
also, Lord, is mercy: for thou renderest
unto man as his activity.

Psalm 63

God, thou art my God; thee I will seek
earnestly: my soul doth thirst for thee,
my flesh doth long for thee in a
dry and thirsty land, of water free;

[2] to behold thy strength and glory, so
in the holy place have seen I thee.
[3] For better is thy mercy than
life; my lips shall give acclaim to thee.

[4] Thus I'll bless thee while I live: in thy
name will I uplift my hands. [5] My soul shall be
sated as with fat and fatness; and my mouth
with joyful lips shall offer praise to thee:

[6] when thee I remember on my bed,
and on thee I, in the watches, meditate.
[7] On account that thou hast been my help, thus in
the shadow of thy wings I'll jubilate.

[8] Hard my soul doth follow after thee:
me thy right hand holdeth up. [9] But those
that for destruction seek my soul,
they shall go into terrestrial lows.

[10] By the sword they'll fall: for foxes they
shall be portions. [11] But the king shall joy in God;
all who swear by him shall glory: but estopped
shall be the mouth of them that utter fraud.

Psalm 64

· God, hear my voice in my complaint: my life
 guard from terror of the enemy.
 ² Hide me from the secret counsel of the wicked; from
 tumult of the workers of iniquity:

· ³ who sharpen like a sword their tongue, and who
 bend their bows to shoot their arrows, yea
 bitter words: ⁴ to shoot in secret at the perfect man:
 suddenly they shoot at him, and fear not they.

⁵ They encourage one another in
 a malicious matter: they concert
 in laying hidden snares;
 Who shall see them? they assert.

⁶ Search they out iniquities; complete
 they a thorough search: the inward part
 of ev'ry one of them
 is profound, as is the heart.

· ⁷ But with an arrow God shall shoot at them;
 wounded in a moment shall be they.
 ⁸ So shall make they their own tongue to fall upon themselves:
 all the ones that look on them shall flee away.

· ⁹ And ev'ry man shall fear and tell God's work;
 for his doing they shall contemplate.
 ¹⁰ In the Lord the righteous shall be glad and trust in him;
 also all the right in heart shall celebrate.

Psalm 65

For thee, O God, in Zion waiteth praise:
and to thee the vow performed shall be.
[2] O thou the one that hearkenest to prayer,
all of flesh shall come to thee.

· [3] Against me matters of iniquities prevail;
thou shalt purge our trespasses away.
[4] The man is bless'd whom thou dost choose
and draw to thee, that in thy courts abide he may:

· we shall be sated with the goodness of thy house,
even with thy temple's holiness.
[5] By fearful things in righteousness,
O God of our salvation, thou wilt answer us;

who art the trust of all the earth's extremes
and them far away upon the sea:
[6] which setteth fast the mountains by his strength,
girded being with mastery:

[7] which quieteth the oceans' roaring, their
billows' noise, the nations' din as well.
[8] And at thy tokens are afraid they that
in the utmost regions dwell:

· the goings out of morn and eve thou makest to
shout in gladness. [9] Thou dost overlook
the earth, and waterest it: thou
enrichest it much. Full of water is God's brook.

Preparest thou them corn, when for it thou
hast provided so. [10] Thou waterest
the ridges thereof to satiety:
thou its furrows settlest:

· with showers makest thou it soft: thou blessest its
springing. [11] Crownest thou with thy largesse
the year; thy pathways also drip
with fatness; [12] drip the pastures of the wilderness:

and little hills rejoice on ev'ry side.
[13] Clothed the pastures are with flocks; with seed
the valleys, too, are covered over; they
shout for joy, they sing indeed.

Psalm 66

^{1} Make a joyful noise to God, ye countries all:
^{2}sing his name's renown: impart
glory in the praise of him. ^{3}Declare to God,
How fearful in thy works thou art!

^{1} Through the greatness of thy power shall thy foes
feign obedience to thee.
^{4}All the earth shall bow and sing to thee; unto
thy name shall make they melody.   *Selah.*

^{5}Come and see God's works: toward the sons of men
he is terrible in deed.
^{6}He converted sea to dry terrain: on foot
they through the river did proceed:

· there did we rejoice in him. ^{7}For ever he
ruleth by his potency;
on the nations look his eyes: let not exalt
themselves the ones refractory.   *Selah.*

^{8}Bless our God, ye people, and
make his praise's voice be heard:
^{9}holdeth he our soul in life,
and he letteth not our feet be stirred.

^{10}For thou, God, hast tested us: us thou hast tried,
as is silver purified.
^{11}Thou hast brought into the net us; thou hast laid
affliction on our hinder side.

^{12}O'er our heads thou hast induced
men to ride; through fire we went,
and through water: but us thou
broughtest to a venue affluent.

^{13}I will go into thy house with off'rings burnt:
pay my vows will I to thee,
^{14}which my lips have uttered and my mouth hath said,
when I was in adversity.

^{15}Offerings of fatlings burnt
I will offer unto thee,
with the incense sweet of rams;
I will offer bullocks with goats-he.   *Selah.*

[16] Come and listen, all that fear
God, and I will testify
what hath done he for my soul.
[17] Unto him I with my mouth did cry,

with my tongue was he extolled
also. [18] If iniquity
I regard within my heart,
then the Lord will hearken not to me:

[19] verily, though, God hath heard me; to the voice
of my prayer hath hearkened he.
[20] Bless'd be God, which hath not turned my prayer away,
nor turned his steadfast love from me.

Psalm 67

· God be merciful to us,
and bless us; cause his face to shine on us;
Selah.
²that thy way may on the earth be known,
in nations all thy saving aid.
³Let the people give thee praise, O God;
let all them give thee accolade.

⁴Let the nations jubilate and sing
for joy: for thou shalt righteously
judge the populace; the nations on
the earth, too, thou shalt oversee.   *Selah.*

⁵Let the people give thee praise, O God;
let all the people give thee laud.
⁶Then the earth shall yield her increase;
and God shall bless us, our own God.

· ⁷God shall bless us; and him fear
shall all the ends of the terrestrial sphere.

Psalm 68

Let God arise and let his foes
dissipated be:
let them also that detest
him before him flee.

$\cdot$ ²Just as smoke is driven off, so drive
them away: as wax doth melt before
fire so at the countenance of God,
let the wicked people be no more.

³But let rejoice the righteous; let
them before God be
jubilant: yea, let them be
glad exceedingly.

$\cdot$ ⁴Sing ye unto God, unto his name
make ye praiseful music: elevate
him that rideth on the heavens; his
name is JAH, before him jubilate.

⁵A father of the fatherless,
also a defense
of the widows: God in his
holy residence.

$\cdot$ ⁶God doth set the solitary in
families: captives which are bound with chain
bringeth out he: but rebellious ones
in a desiccated land remain.

⁷O God, when wentest thou in front
of thy populace,
at the time that thou didst march
through the wilderness;   *Selah*:

$\cdot$ ⁸quiver did the earth, the heavens, too,
dropped before the face of God: as well
Sinai was itself commoved at the
face of God, the God of Israel.

⁹O God, thou sprinkledst a rain
plentiful, whereby
thine inheritance, when tired,
thou didst certify.

¹⁰Thy congregation hath therein
settled: thou, O God,
of thy goodness hast prepared
for him undertrod.

¹¹Give the order did the Lord: immense
was the host of those that tidings bore.
¹²Kings of armies fled: and she that at
home remained divided spoils of war.

¹³Though ye have reclined among the pots,
nonetheless ye shall be as the wings
of a dove bespread with silver and,
topped with yellow gold, her featherings.

¹⁴When th'Almighty scattered kings in it,
as the snow in Salmon it was white.
¹⁵As is Bashan's hill, the hill of God;
as is Bashan's hill a hill of height.

¹⁶Why leap ye, O ye lofty hills?
God doth wish to sit
in this hill; yea, ever will
dwell the LORD in it.

¹⁷Twenty thousand are God's chariots,
thousands upon thousands, verily:
in their midst the Lord is, just as in
Sinai, in the holy place, is he.

¹⁸Thou hast risen to the height, thou hast
captured captives: thou hast seized for men
gifts; yea, for the rebels also, that
YAHWEH God might dwell among them then.

¹⁹The Lord be blessèd, he who doth
with benevolence
daily load us, God who is
our deliverance.   *Selah.*

²⁰Our God is he that's God unto
salvatory feats;
and to GOD the Lord belong
death's egressive metes.

²¹But God shall wound the head of his
foes, the hairy pate
of the one who goeth on
in his guilty state.

²²The Lord said, From Bashan will I
bring them yet once more;
from the bottoms of the sea,
them will I restore:

²³that in the blood of enemies
may be dipped thy foot,
and that in the same may thy
canines' tongue be put.

²⁴Thy processions they have seen, O God;
yea, the goings of my God, my King,
in the sanctuary. ²⁵Singers went
on before, musicians following;

in the midst of them producing tune
on the timbrels were the damosels.
²⁶In the choirs bless ye God, the Lord
even, from the fount of Israel.

²⁷There is little Benjamin, their chief;
dukes of Judah and their company;
in addition, dukes of Zebulun;
furthermore, the dukes of Naphtali.

²⁸Charged thy power hath thy God: O God,
that which thou hast wrought for us make strong.
²⁹From thy temple at Jerusalem,
kings to thee shall carry gifts along.

³⁰Rebuke the animal of the
reed, the multitude
of the bulls, along with the
peoples' bovine brood,

till ev'ry one with silver bits
doth himself prostrate:
people that delight in war
do thou dissipate.

^{31}Out of Egypt, princes shall arrive;
Cush shall stretch her hands to God out soon.
^{32}Sing to God, ye kingdoms of the earth;
make unto the Lord a praiseful tune;   *Selah*:

^{33}to the rider on the heavens of
heavens, which were of antiquity;
contemplate, he sendeth out his voice,
and it is a voice of potency.

^{34}Ascribe ye power unto God:
over Israel
is his grandeur; in the clouds
is his strength as well.

^{35}From thy holy places, God, thou art
feared: the God of Israel is he
that unto his people doth bestow
fortitude and power. Bless'd God be.

Psalm 69

· Save thou me, O God; for come unto my soul
the waters are.[2] I sink in mire deep,
where there's no standing: I am come to depths
of waters, where the floods me oversweep.

·[3] I am weary of my crying: dried's my throat:
mine eyes consume while for my God I wait.
[4] More numerous than hairs upon my head
are they that me gratuitously hate:

· they that would destroy me, being wrongfully
my foes, are mighty: then restore I did
what stole I not.[5] O God, my foolishness
thou knowest; and my sins from thee aren't hid.

·[6] Let not them that wait expectantly on thee,
Lord GOD of hosts, be shamed because of me:
O God of Israel, let not the ones
that seek thee be confused because of me.

·[7] For on thine account, reproach have borne I; shame
hath blanketed my face.[8] I am become
an alien unto my brethren, and
a stranger to the children of my mum.

·[9] For the zeal of thy house hath me devoured;
and scornings of the ones that chided thee
on me are fallen.[10] When I wept, my soul
with fasting, 'twas to the reproach of me.

·[11] And I made my garment sackcloth; also I
became a proverb unto them.[12] Complain
against me do the sitters in the gate;
and of the drunkards I was the refrain.

·[13] But as for myself, my prayer is unto thee,
O LORD, in season of benevolence:
O God, in greatness of thy mercy hear
me, in the truth of thy deliverance.

·[14] From the mire, deliver me; let not me sink:
from them that hate me let me rescued be,
and from the waters deep.[15] Let not the flood
engulf me, let the deep not swallow me,

· and let not the pit upon me shut her mouth.
^{16}Lord, hear me; for thy mercy is benign:
according to the multitude of thy
compassions tender unto me incline.

^{17}And conceal from thy servant not thy face;
for I'm in trouble: quickly answer me.
^{18}Approach thou nigh my soul, redeem it: on
account of mine opponents, ransom me.

^{19}My reproach, and shame, and insult thou hast known:
in front of thee are ev'ry one of my
antagonists. ^{20}Contumely hath broke
my heart; and full of heaviness am I:

· and I looked for sympathy, but there was none;
for comforters as well, but found I nil.
^{21}And for my meat they gave me gall; and in
my thirst they gave me vinegar to swill.

^{22}Before them let their table
come to be a gin:
and let become a trap what for
their welfare should have been.

^{23}Let their eyes be darkened, that they see not; and
continually make their loins to shake.
^{24}Upon them pour thine indignation, and
let hold of them thy wrathful anger take.

^{25}Let be desolate their habitation; and
let no one dwell within their tents. ^{26}For stalk
they him whom thou hast smote; and to the grief
of those whom thou hast wounded do they talk.

^{27}Add iniquity to their iniquity:
and in thy righteousness let come them not.
^{28}Let them be blotted from the book of life,
and with the righteous ones be written not.

^{29}Also I am poor and sorrowful: O God,
let thy salvation settle me on high.
^{30}Acclaim the name of God will I in song,
and with thanksgiving him I'll magnify.

³¹ Also this shall please JEHOVAH better than
an ox or bullock, horned and cloven-pawed.
³² The humble ones shall see this, and be glad:
your heart shall live if ye inquire of God.

³³ For the LORD doth hear the paupers, and doth not
despise his prisoners. ³⁴ Let give him laud
the heav'n and earth, the seas, and all that move
therein. ³⁵ For saved will Zion be by God,

also Judah's cities will construct he: that
may dwell there they, and have it occupied.
³⁶ Possess it also shall his servants' seed:
and they that love his name shall there abide.

Psalm 70

· Hasten to deliver me, O God;
hasten thou, O Lord, to succour me.
²Let them that seek to take my soul
disconcerted and confounded be:

· let them to the rear be turned and put
to confusion that desire my maim.
³Let them that say, Aha, aha,
be reversed as wages of their shame.

⁴Let all of those that seek thee be
glad and in thee jubilate:
and let thy salvation's lovers say
continually, God is great.

·⁵Also I am poor and destitute:
hasten unto me, O God: mine aid
and my deliverer art thou;
O Jehovah, be thou not delayed.

Psalm 71

¹ Lord, in thee, I put my trust: let me be not
ever to confusion put. ²Deliver me
in thy righteousness, and cause me to escape:
unto me incline thine ear, and save thou me.

³Be to me a rock, a dwelling
whereunto I alway may resort:
thou hast given a commandment to
save me; for thou art my rock and fort.

⁴O my God, deliver thou me from the hand
of the wicked, from the hand of the unjust
and the cruel. ⁵For thou art my hope, Lord God:
from my juvenility thou art my trust.

⁶I by thee have been upholden
from the matrix: thou didst sever me
from the bowels of my mother: my
praise shall be continually of thee.

⁷I am as a wonder unto
many; but thou art my refuge strong.
⁸Let my mouth be filled with thine acclaim,
also with thine honor all day long.

⁹Cast me not away in time of agedness;
when my vigor faileth do not me forsake.
¹⁰For mine enemies against me chatter; and
watchers of my soul together counsel take,

¹¹saying, God hath him forsaken: persecute
and arrest ye him; for there is nobody
to deliver him. ¹²O God, from me be not
distant: hasten, O my God, to succor me.

¹³Let them that are adversaries
to my soul ashamed and wasted be;
with reproach and with dishonor let
them be clad that seek mine injury.

¹⁴But I'll hope continually, and I'll yet
praise thee more and more. ¹⁵My mouth shall tell of thy
righteousness and thy salvation all the day;
for their numerations do not fathom I.

⋅¹⁶In the Lord JEHOVAH's power I will go:
I will cite thy righteousness, yea thine alone.
¹⁷Thou, O God, hast taught me from my youth: and thy
wondrous doings hitherto have made I known.

¹⁸Also now when I am old and
grayhaired, God, forsake me not; until
I have showed thy strength unto this age,
and thy pow'r to all them coming still.

⋅¹⁹And thy righteousness, O God, is very high,
who hast done stupendous things: O God, to thee
who is like!²⁰Thou, which hast showed me great and sore
tribulations, shalt again enliven me,

⋅ and shalt bring me up again from depths of the
earth.²¹Thou shalt increase my greatness, and shalt me
comfort all around.²²Moreover, I will praise
thee (indeed thy truth), my God, with psaltery:

⋅ unto thee will I deliver melody
with the harp, thou Holy One of Israel.
²³When I sing to thee my lips shall shout for joy;
and my soul, the which thou hast redeemed, as well.

²⁴Of thy righteousness, moreover,
the entire day my tongue shall speak:
for they are confounded, for they are
disconcerted, that mine evil seek.

Psalm 72

Give the king, O God, thy judgments and
to the scion of the king thy righteousness.
^{2}With righteousness thy people shall he judge,
and with equity thy penniless.

^{3}Carry peace unto the people shall the mountains, and
the hills, by righteousness. ^{4}The people's destitute
he shall judge, the children of the needy one
he shall save, and the oppressor he shall comminute.

^{5}As the sun and moon continue on,
unto generations all shall fear they thee.
^{6}Like rain on meadow mown, as showers that
irrigate the earth, descend shall he.

^{7}Flourish shall the righteous in his days; and multitude
of peace until the moon no more endureth. ^{8}And
he shall exercise command from sea to sea,
also from the river to the limits of the land.

^{9}Nomads that abide within the wilderness shall bow
before him; lick the dust, too, shall his enemies.
^{10}Kings of Tarshish and the isles shall render gifts:
kings of Sheba and Seba shall bring gratuities.

^{11}Yea, before him all the kings shall bow:
nations all shall serve him. ^{12}For the needy he
shall rescue when he crieth; and the poor,
who hath to assist him nobody.

^{13}He shall spare the poor and needy and
save the souls of needy ones. ^{14}Their soul shall he
redeem from fraud and violence: as well,
precious in his sight their blood shall be.

^{15}He shall live, and unto him shall be
given of the gold of Sheba: also they
shall make continually prayer for him;
he shall be saluted all the day.

^{16}In the earth shall be a handful of
corn upon the mountaintops; its fruit shall roil
like Lebanon: and they of city shall
flourish like the herbage of the soil.

[17] Evermore continue shall his name:
multiplied before the sun shall be his name:
and bless'd in him shall be humanity:
bless'd shall all the nations him proclaim.

[18] Blessed be JEHOVAH God, the God of Israel,
who only doeth wondrous things. [19] And ever be
bless'd the name of his renown: and let be filled
all the world with his glory. So be, and so be.
[20] Ended are the prayers of David, son of Jesse.

Book III

Psalm 73

1. Truly God is good to Israel, to
even such as are of clear
heart. 2. But as for me, my feet were almost gone;
yea, my steps had slipped well near.

3. For toward the foolish I was jealous,
when the wicked people's peace
I beheld. 4. For in their death there are no bands:
and their belly is obese.

5. They are not in toil as other men;
nor like other men are stricken they.
6. Thus as a chain doth pride encompass them;
as a garment, violence doth them array.

7. Out with fatness stand their eyeballs: they have
more than heart could wish. 8. They mock,
and about oppression speak they wickedly:
from the altitude they talk.

9. Set against the heavens they their mouth,
also through the earth doth walk their tongue.
10. And so return his people hither: and
out to them are waters of abundance wrung.

11. And they say, How knoweth God? And is
any knowledge in the One Most High?
12. Behold, these are the wicked ones at ease
in the world; in opulence, they multiply.

13. Surely I in vain have cleansed my heart,
and have washed my hands in purity.
14. For all the day have I been stricken, and
ev'ry morning bringeth a reproof of me.

15. If I say, I thus will speak; behold,
then I should behave with treachery
against the generation of thy sons.
16. When I thought to know this, it was toil for me;

17. till I went into God's sanctuary;
at that time their final state
understood I. 18. Surely thou in slippery
places didst them situate:

down into destruction thou them castedst.
¹⁹How they're momentarily
into desolation brought! With terrors they
are consumed entirely.

²⁰ As a dream when one awaketh; so when
thou awakest, thou, O Lord,
shalt despise their image.²¹ Thus my heart was grieved,
and I in my reins was gored.

²²I so foolish was, and ignorant:
I was as an animal with thee.
²³Continually, though, am I with thee:
by my right hand thou hast taken hold of me.

²⁴Thou shalt guide me with thy counsel, and
afterward receive to glory me.
²⁵In heaven whom have I but thee? And there's
nothing on the earth that I desire with thee.

²⁶Though the flesh and heart of me consumeth,
God's the fortress of my heart,
and my portion evermore.²⁷ For, lo, they shall
perish that from thee depart:

all of them that go a whoring from
thee thou hast destroyed.²⁸ But to draw nigh
to God is good for me: I've made the Lord
GOD my hope, that number all thy works may I.

Psalm 74

· God, why hast thou for ever cast us off?
Why doth thine anger smoke against the fold
of thy pasturage? ²Remember thy
congregation thou hast bought of old;

· the rod of thine inheritance thou hast
redeemed; this mountain Zion, residence
wherein thou hast taken. ³Lift thy feet
to the ravages of permanence;

· to all the enemy hath wickedly
accomplished in the sanctuary. ⁴Thine
enemies in thine assemblies' midst
roar; they set their ensigns up for signs.

· ⁵According as he'd lifted axes on
a copse of trees, a man was famous. ⁶But
now with ax and hammer, all at once,
break they down its woodwork finely cut.

⁷Into thy sanctuary they've
cast a fiery flame,
to the ground they've sullied the
dwelling of thy name.

⁸They said within their heart, Let us
them together raze:
all God's synagogues in the
land they've set ablaze.

⁹Our tokens see we not: there is
no more any seer:
none that knoweth yet how long
is among us here.

· ¹⁰God, how long shall the adversary scorn?
For ever shall the foe blaspheme thy name?
¹¹Why withdrawest thou thy hand, yea thy
right hand? From thy bosom pluck the same.

· ¹²For God my King is of aforetime; he
doth work salvation in the world's midst.
¹³By thy strength thou didst divide the sea:
break in waters monsters' heads thou didst.

[14.] The dragon's heads thou shatteredst
into pieces, and
gavest him as meat to them
of the desert land.

[15.] Thou didst divide the fountain and the flood:
thou driedst up the streams that ever run.
[16.] Day is thine, moreover night is thine:
thou hast stablished both the light and sun.

[17.] Thou hast established all the bounds of earth
and made the summer and the winter. [18.] LORD,
this recall: the foe hath censured, and
foolish people have thy name abhorred.

[19.] Deliver over not the person of
thy turtledove unto the multitude
of the beasts: forget not evermore
the assembly of thy ones subdued.

[20.] Attend unto the covenant:
for the places dim
of the earth with houses of
barbarism brim.

[21.] Let not return ashamed the one oppressed:
let praise thy name the poor and beggarly.
[22.] Rise, God, plead thy cause: remember how
all the day the fool reproacheth thee.

[23.] Forget thou not the voice of thy
foes: continually
doth increase the tumult of
those withstanding thee.

Psalm 75

To thee, God, do we give acclaim,
do we give acclaim:
that thy name is near do thy
wondrous works proclaim.

²When the time appointed I shall take,
I will rightly judge. ³The world and
all the persons that therein abide
are dissolved: its pillars make I stand.
                                    Selah.
⁴Said I to the boasters, Boast ye not:
and unto the wicked ones, Uplift
not the horn: ⁵do not uplift your horn
to the height or speak with neck that's stiff.

⁶For not from the east, nor from the west,
nor the south doth come promotion. ⁷Yet
God's the judge: he layeth this one low,
and another he doth highly set.

⁸For in JEHOVAH's hand's a cup,
and the wine is red;
it is full of mixture; and
poureth he from said:

but the sediments thereof — them all
wicked persons of the earth shall wring
out and drink. ⁹But ever I'll declare;
praises unto Jacob's God I'll sing.

¹⁰And all the horns of wicked ones —
cut them off will I;
horns, though, of the righteous one
shall be lifted high.

Psalm 76

Renowned is God in Judah; his
name is great in Israel.
² And in Salem is his den, and in
Zion is his place to dwell.

³ There he brake the arrows of the bow,
the shield, and the sword, the war also.
Selah.
⁴ More glorious and excellent
art thou than the hills of prey.
⁵ Plundered are the valiant of heart,
slumbered in their sleep have they:

and found their hands have none of the
men of might. ⁶ O Jacob's God,
chariot and horse, at thy rebuke,
off to heavy slumber nod.

⁷ Thou thyself art one that's fearsome: and
upon thy wrath before thee who may stand?

⁸ From heav'n thou madest judgment be
heard; the earth was frightened and
stilled, ⁹ when rose to judgment God, to save
all the humble of the land.   *Selah.*

¹⁰ For shall praise thee fury of mankind:
the residue of fury thou shalt bind.

¹¹ Unto your God Jehovah vow,
also pay: let all them being
round about him carry presents to
him that should be frightening.

¹² Off the princes' spirit he shall shear:
unto the kings of earth, he's one to fear.

Psalm 77

· With my voice I cried aloud to God,
even with my voice to God; and he
gave unto me ear. ²I sought the Lord
in the day of mine adversity:

· in the night my sore discharged, and ceased
not: consoled my soul refused to be.
³I remembered God, and moaned: complained
I, and faint the spirit was of me.   *Selah.*

·⁴Thou dost hold mine eyelids open: I
am so troubled that I cannot speak.
⁵I have thought upon the days of old,
mindful of the years of times antique.

⁶In the night my song
I recall to memory:
I commune with mine own heart;
my spirit quested thoroughly.

⁷Will the Lord reject
evermore? And will not he
favor any longer? ⁸Is
his mercy gone eternally?

Doth his promise fail
to all generations? ⁹Hath
God forgotten graciousness?
His mercies hath he stopped in wrath? *Selah.*

¹⁰And I said, This is
mine infirmity: but I
will to mind recall the years
of the right hand of the most High.

¹¹I will call to mind
YAHWEH's doings: certainly
I will bring to memory
thy wonders of antiquity.

·¹²I will also ponder all thy work,
and upon thy doings meditate.
¹³God, thy way is in the holy place:
who is, as our God, a God so great?

[14] Thou, the God that doest wonders, hast
in the nations shown thy potency,
[15] and with arm redeemed thy people, of
Jacob and of Joseph progeny.　　　　*Selah.*

[16] God, the waters saw thee, saw thee the
waters; they were anguished: the profound
places, too, were troubled. [17] Poured the clouds
water out: the skies emitted sound:

· furthermore thine arrows here and there
went. [18] Within the whirlwind was the sound
of thy thunder: lightnings lightened the
world: shake and tremble did the ground.

[19] In the sea thy way, thy path in great
waters, and thy footsteps are not kenned.
[20] Thou didst, by the hand of Moses and
Aaron, like a flock thy people tend.

Psalm 78

· Give thou ear, my people, to my law: incline your ears
to the sayings of my mouth.² My mouth I'll open wide
in verse: I'll utter riddles dark of old:³ which we
have heard and known; our fathers have us told beside.

⁴From their sons will not we hide them, narrating
to the coming generation the
laudations of JEHOVAH, and his strength, and his
wondrous doings that performed hath he.

⁵For in Jacob he a testimony raised,
and in Israel appointed he
a law, which charged he to our fathers, that they should
make them known unto their progeny:

· ⁶so that the succeeding generation might them know,
children to be born; who should arise and them declare
unto their sons:⁷ that they might set their hope in God,
and not forget God's works, but for his precepts care:

⁸and not as their fathers be: an obdurate
generation, one rebellious, too;
a generation that established not their heart,
and whose spirit was with God untrue.

⁹Sons of Ephraim, being armed, and carrying
bows, in day of battle did withdraw.
¹⁰The covenant of God they kept not, and refused
they to walk according to his law;

¹¹and forgat his doings, and his miracles
that them he had showed.¹² Astounding deed
he did within the vision of their ancestors,
in the land of Egypt, Zoan's mead.

¹³Parted he the sea, and through it made them pass;
and he made the waters stand upright
in heap.¹⁴ He also led them with a cloud by day,
and a light of fire all the night.

¹⁵In the wilderness he clave the rocks, and gave
drink as from abundant depths.¹⁶ Also,
educed he fluids from the craggy rock and caused
waters to, like rivers, downward flow.

[17] Yet continued they to sin against him still
by provoking in the arid dust
the Highest. [18] And they put God to the test in their
heart by asking meat unto their lust.

[19] They, indeed, against God spake; they said, Can God arrange
in the wilderness a table? [20] Lo, the rock he beat,
that waters gushed, and overflowed the streams; can bread
he also give? Can he provide his people meat?

[21] Therefore did JEHOVAH hear this, and was livid: so
fire was in Jacob kindled, also anger hot
arose on Israel; [22] for they did not believe
in God, and they in his salvation trusted not:

[23] though the clouds he had commanded from above,
and had opened wide the doors of heav'n,
[24] and had upon them showered manna down to eat,
and had giv'n them of the corn of heav'n.

[25] Man did eat the angels' food: he sent them meat
to the full. [26] He made an east wind gust
from heav'n: and by his pow'r, he brought the south wind in.
[27] Also rained he flesh on them as dust,

even feathered flyers as the sand of seas;
[28] make it fall within their camp did he,
around their dwellings. [29] So they ate, and were well filled:
for he gave them their cupidity;

[30] from their lust they weren't estranged. But while their meat
was yet in their mouths, [31] upon them fell
the wrath of God; he slew their fattest, and he smote
down the chosen men of Israel.

[32] Yet for all this still they sinned, and trusted not in his
wonders. [33] So their days did he consume in vanity,
and years in dread. [34] When slew them he, then sought him they:
and they returned and quested for God earnestly.

[35] And recalled they that their rock was God, and that
their redeemer was the God most high.
[36] They nonetheless did flatter with their mouth him, and
with their tongues they unto him did lie.

[37] For with him their heart was not aright, and not
steadfast in his covenant were they.
[38] But their iniquity forgave he, being of
mercy full, and waste he did not lay:

many times, indeed, he turned his wrath away,
and he roused not all his fury hot.
[39] For he remembered that they were but flesh; a wind
that departeth, and returneth not.

[40] How they oft provoked him in the desert! They
grieved him in the wilderness as well.
[41] Yea, they returned and tempted God, and limited
they the Holy One of Israel.

[42] They remembered not his power, nor the day
when he from the enemy them freed.
[43] How he in Egypt had performed his signs and his
deeds miraculous in Zoan's mead:

[44] how he had transformed their rivers into blood;
and their floods, that not imbibe could they.
[45] He sent among them varied sorts of flies, which ate
them; and frogs, which waste to them did lay.

[46] And unto the caterpillar gave he their
increase, and unto the locust tossed
their labor. [47] Devastated he their vines with hail,
and their sycamores he killed with frost.

[48] Furthermore he gave their cattle up unto the hail,
and their flocks to bolts of lightning. [49] Unto them he sent
the fierceness of his anger, wrath, and fury, and
distress, by sending messengers malevolent.

[50] To his wrath he made a way; he spared not their
soul from death, but to the pestilence
surrendered he their life; [51] and smote in Egypt all
firstborn; chief of strength within Ham's tents:

[52] but he made his people to proceed like sheep,
and within the wilderness he led
them like a flock. [53] And in security them he
guided, so that they were not in dread:

but the ones who were their enemies the sea
overwhelmed.[54] Moreover them he brought
unto the border of his sanctuary, yea
to this mountain his right hand had bought.

[55] Furthermore he cast the heathen out before
them, and he divided them by line
a heritage, moreover in their tents did he
make the tribes of Israel recline.

[56] Yet they tempted and provoked the God Supreme,
and kept not his testimonies:[57] but
turned back, and dealt covertly like their fathers: they
twisted like a bow inaccurate.

[58] For to anger they provoked him with their high
places, and they moved to jealousy
him with their carvings.[59] When God heard, he angered, and
loathed he Israel exceedingly:

[60] so that he forsook the tent of Shiloh, the
tent which he had placed in humans;[61] and
he gave his strength into captivity, and his
glory into the opponent's hand.

[62] And he gave his people over to the sword;
and was with his heritage irate.
[63] The fire consumed their adolescent men; and their
maidens came not into married state.

[64] By the broadsword fell their priests; their widows yet
made no lamentation.[65] Then as out
of sleep the Lord awakened, like a mighty man
that by consequence of wine doth shout.

[66] And he smote his enemies in hinder parts:
he appointed them to endless jibe.
[67] Moreover he refused the tabernacle of
Joseph, and he chose not Ephraim's tribe:

[68] but he chose the tribe of Judah, mountain Zion which
loved he.[69] And he built his sanctum like the places steep,
as earth which he hath ever stablished.[70] And he chose
his servant David, and him took from folds of sheep:

⁷¹him he brought from trailing ewes with young to shepherd his people Jacob, and his heirloom Israel. ⁷²So he them fed according to his heart's integrity;
and them he guided by his hands' dexterity.

Psalm 79

Into thine inheritance, O God,
infidels are come; they have defiled
thy holy temple; they in heaps
Jerusalem have piled.

² Corpses of thy servants have, as meat,
given they to flyers heavenly;
to earthly animals the flesh
of holy ones of thee.

³ They have shed their blood like water round about
Jerusalem; and burying was nobody.
⁴ To our neighbors a reproach are we become,
to them that compass us a scorn and mockery.

⁵ How long, O JEHOVAH? Wilt thou be enraged
for ever? Shall thy jealousy combust like flame?
⁶ Pour thy wrath on nations that have known thee not,
and on the realms that have not called upon thy name.

⁷ For they have devoured Jacob; laid they waste
his dwelling place. ⁸ Against us, O remember not
past iniquities: let meet us speedily
thy tender mercies: for we very low are brought.

⁹ Help us, God of our salvation, by
reason of the glory of thy name:
and rescue us, and purge our sins,
for purpose of thy fame.

¹⁰ Why should nations question, Where's their God?
Let him in our sight be known throughout
the nations by the vengeance for
thy servants' blood poured out.

¹¹ Let the pris'ner's sighing come before
thee; as to the greatness of thine arm,
preserve alive the ones that are
condemned to fatal harm;

¹² render thou, moreover, sevenfold
to our neighbors their contumely
into their bosom, wherewith have
reproached, O Lord, they thee.

¹³Therefore we thy people and the sheep
of thy pasture will thee thank always:
to generations all will we
enumerate thy praise.

Psalm 80

Give thou ear, O Shepherd of
Israel, thou that dost guide
Joseph like a flock; forth shine thou that
dost between the cherubim abide.

[2] In front of Ephraim and Benjamin
and Manasseh stir thou up thy potency,
and come and save us. [3] Turn again us, God,
and cause thy face to shine; and saved shall we then be.

[4] JEHOVAH God of hosts, how long against
thine own people's prayer wilt thou remain irate?
[5] Thou makest them to eat the bread of tears;
and givest tears to them to drink in measure great.

[6] Unto our neighbors, us thou makest strife:
also ridicule us those at enmity
with us. [7] Again us turn, O God of hosts,
and cause thy face to shine; and saved shall we then be.

[8] From out of Egypt thou hast brought a vine:
thou hast driven out the heathen nations, and
hast planted it. [9] The ground preparedst thou
before it, and it rooted deep and filled the land.

[10] The hills were covered with the shade of it,
and her boughs were like the cedar trees of God.
[11] She sent her branches out unto the sea,
and to the river she her branches sent abroad.

[12] Why hast thou broken down her hedges, so
all them pluck her which along the way do pass?
[13] The feral boar from wood doth waste it, and
devour it doth the wild mammal of the grass.

[14] Return, thee we beseech, O God of hosts:
look from heaven down, and watch, and oversee
this vine; [15] the vineyard, too, which thy right hand
hath planted, and the branch thou madest strong for thee.

[16] It's burned with fire, it's sickled: at rebuke
of thy countenance they are destroyed. [17] Let be
thy hand upon the man of thy right hand,
upon the son of man thou madest strong for thee.

¹⁸ And then from thee will turn we not away:
quicken us, then call upon thy name will we.
¹⁹ Again us turn, JEHOVAH God of hosts,
and cause thy face to shine; and saved shall we then be.

Psalm 81

Sing aloud ye unto God our strength: unto
the God of Jacob shout ye joyfully.
²Uplift a psalm, and bring the timbrel hither ye,
the pleasant lyre with the psaltery.

³Blow the trumpet monthly, when the moon is new,
on festal day of our solemnity.
⁴Because this was for Israel a statute; of
the God of Jacob, it was a decree.

⁵For a testimony he appointed this
in Joseph, when he went throughout the land
of Egypt, a locality in which I heard
a language that I did not understand.

⁶I took away his shoulder from the burden: from the pots,
delivered were his hands. ⁷Thou calledst in adversity,
and thee I delivered; in the thunder's secret place
I answered thee: at waters of Meribah proved I thee.   *Selah.*

⁸O my people, hear and I will testify
to thee: O Israel, if to me thou
wilt hearken; ⁹there shall be no other god in thee;
nor shalt to any foreign god thou bow.

¹⁰I'm the LORD thy God, which brought thee from the land
of Egypt: open wide thy mouth, and I
will fill it. ¹¹But my people would not hear my voice;
and Israel would not with me comply.

¹²So to their stubborn hearts I gave them up: they walked in their
own counsels. ¹³That my people unto me had hearkened, and
Israel had walked within my ways! ¹⁴I should have soon
subdued their foes, and on their adversaries turned my hand.

¹⁵The haters of JEHOVAH unto him should have themselves
submitted: but their time should have endured eternally.
¹⁶And he should have fed them with the finest of the wheat:
with honey from the rock I should have also sated thee.

Psalm 82

[1] God standeth in the council of divinity;
adjudgeth he among the gods. [2] How long
will ye judge unjustly, and accept
partially the persons of the doers wrong? *Selah.*

[3] Defend the poor and fatherless: do justice to
the one afflicted and the beggarly.
[4] Rescue ye the poor and needy one:
from the hand of persons wicked, rid them ye.

[5] They neither know, nor will they understand; they walk
in darkness: all the earth's foundations lie
out of course. [6] I've stated, Ye are gods;
all of you are children of the One Most High.

[7] But ye shall die like men, and like
one of the princes fall.
[8] Arise, O God, adjudge the earth:
for thou shalt inherit nations all.

Psalm 83

1. Keep, O God, not silence: hold not thy
   peace, O God, and be thou not sedate.
2. For, behold, thine enemies a tumult make:
   and raised the head have persons that thee hate.

3. Counsel shrewd against thy people have
   taken they, and they've conspiracy
   formed against thy hidden persons. 4. Come, they've said,
   let's cut them off from nationality;

that the name of Israel may not
any more be held in memory.
5. For together have consulted they with one
   consent: they've made a league, opposed to thee:

6. Edom's tents, the Ishmaelites as well;
   Moab, furthermore the Hagarenes;
7. Gebal, and Ammon, Amalek also; with
   inhabitants of Tyre, the Philistines;

8. with them is Assur also tied:
   the sons of Lot they've fortified.   *Selah.*

9. Do to them as unto Midian;
   as to Sisera, and Jabin, at
   waterway of Kison: 10. which were overthrown
   at Endor: for the earth became they scat.

11. Make their dukes like Oreb and Ze'eb:
    yea, as Zebah all their princes make,
    and as Zalmunna: 12. who said, Unto ourselves
    possession of God's houses let us take.

13. Make them, O my God, like whirling chaff;
    as the stubble in the face of gust.
14. As the fire burneth up a forest, and
    as flame doth make the mountains to combust;

15. so with thy tempest them pursue;
    alarm them with thy whirlwind, too.

16. Their countenances fill with shame;
    that they, O Lord, may seek thy name.

[17] Let them be for ever shamed and vexed;
let them, yea, be put to shame, and die:
[18] so they know that over all the earth thou, by
thy name JEHOVAH, art alone most high.

Psalm 84

How amiable, LORD of hosts,
are thy tabernacles! ²For
JEHOVAH's courts my soul doth long,
consumeth even, furthermore:

my heart and flesh exclaim to the
living God. ³The sparrow, yea,
hath found a house, and swallow her
a nest, where lay her young she may,

beside thine altars even, O
LORD of hosts, my King and God.
⁴Indwellers of thy house are bless'd:
to thee they'll still be giving laud.   *Selah.*

· ⁵Blessed is the man whose strength's in thee;
in whose heart the ways of them are. ⁶Who
passing through the vale of weeping make the place
a well; the rain doth fill the pools, too.

· ⁷They proceed from strength to strength, and each
one of them in Zion doth appear
unto God. ⁸O YAHWEH God of armies, hear
my prayer: O God of Jacob, give thou ear.   *Selah.*

⁹Behold, O God our shield, and look
on thy one anointed's face.
¹⁰For better's one day in thy courts
than thousand in another place.

· I had rather be a doorkeeper
in the dwelling of my God, than live
in the sinners' tents. ¹¹For YAHWEH God is sun
and shield: the LORD will grace and glory give:

no good will he withhold from them
that proceed in probity.
¹²O LORD of hosts, how blessèd is
the man that placeth trust in thee.

Psalm 85

· Favor thou hast shown, LORD, to thy land:
  the captivity of Jacob thou hast brought again.
²Thou hast pardoned the iniquity of thy
  people, thou hast covered over all their sin.   *Selah.*

·³Thou hast taken all thy wrath away:
  thou hast turned thyself from fierceness of thine angry state.
⁴Turn thou us, O God of our salvation, and
  cause thine anger us toward to terminate.

·⁵Wilt thou be for ever cross with us?
  Wilt to ages all extend thou thy lividity?
⁶Wilt thou not revivify us once again:
  that thy people may be jubilant in thee?

·⁷Show us, LORD, thy mercy and us grant
  thy salvation. ⁸I will hear what God the LORD will say:
  for unto his people and his saints he'll speak
  peace: but turn again to folly must not they.

·⁹Surely his salvation is to his
  fearers nigh; that in our country, glory may persist.
¹⁰Truth and lovingkindness are together met;
  righteousness and peace have one another kissed.

¹¹Truth shall spring up from the earth; also
  righteousness from heav'n shall look below.

¹²Yea, the LORD shall give the good thing; and
  yield up her increase shall our land.

¹³Righteousness shall go before his face;
  and shall in his footsteps' way us place.

Psalm 86

¹ Incline thine ear, O Lord, me hear:
for I am poor and beggarly.
²Preserve my soul; for I am holy: thou my God,
save thy servant that doth trust in thee.

³Be merciful to me, O Lord:
for unto thee I daily cry.
⁴Exhilarate thy servant's soul: because, O Lord,
elevate my soul to thee do I.

⁵For thou art good and sparing, Lord,
and in clemency
plenteous to all of the
ones that call on thee.

⁶Lord, give thou ear unto my prayer;
and hearken to the voice of my
entreaties. ⁷I will call on thee in day of my
trouble: for to me thou wilt reply.

⁸Among the gods, O Lord, there is
like unto thee none;
neither like unto thy works
is there even one.

⁹The nations all, whom thou hast made,
shall before thee, Lord,
come and bow; and glory they'll
to thy name accord.

¹⁰For thou art great, and wondrous things
thou doest: God alone thou art.
¹¹Direct me in thy way, Lord; I will walk in thy
truth: to fear thy name, unite my heart.

¹²O Lord my God, thee I will give
praise with all of my
heart: and evermore thy name
I will glorify.

¹³For great thy lovingkindness is
me toward: as well,
thou hast snatched my soul away
from the lowest hell.

¹⁴O God, the proud are risen up
on me, and for my soul have sought
assemblies of the practicers of violence;
and before them they have set thee not.

¹⁵But, Lord, a God compassionate
art thou, gracious, too,
slow of wrath, and ample in
mercy, also true.

¹⁶O turn to me, and have on me
mercy; to thy slave
give thy strength; the son of thine
handmaid also save.

¹⁷Prepare with me a sign for good;
that they which hate me may it see,
and be ashamed: because, JEHOVAH, thou hast helped
me, and thou hast consolated me.

Psalm 87

· His foundation's in the holy hills.
²Yahweh loveth gates of Zion far
above the dwellings all of Jacob. ³City of
God, of thee things glorious reported are.					*Selah.*

·⁴Mention I will make of Rahab and
Babylon unto my knowers: see
Philistia, and Tyre, with Ethiopia;
born this person was in that locality.

·⁵And of Zion shall be said, In her
born was this and that man: and prepare
her shall the One Supreme.⁶The Lord shall count, when he
writeth up the people, Born was this one there.		*Selah.*

⁷And the singers, as the pipers, there shall be:
all my fountains are in thee.

Psalm 88

Yahweh, God of my deliverance,
cried before thee day and night have I:
²before thy face let come my prayer:
incline thine ear unto my cry;

·³for my soul is full of troubles: and
to the grave my life advanceth nigh.
⁴I am counted with the ones that to the pit
plummet: as a man that hath no strength am I:

⁵free among the lifeless, like the ones
slain that in the sepulchre do lay,
whom thou rememberest no more:
and from thy hand are severed they.

⁶Thou hast laid me in the lowest pit,
in the darkness, in the parts profound.
⁷Upon me lieth hard thy wrath,
and thou with all thy waves hast downed. *Selah.*

⁸Mine acquaintance thou hast put away
far from me; a thing of odium
to them me thou hast rendered: I'm
restricted; forth I cannot come.

·⁹Mine eye mourneth on account of woe:
daily, Lord, I've called on thee, to thee
I have spread my hands.¹⁰Wilt show thou miracles
to the dead? Shall ghosts arise? Shall praise they thee?
Selah.
·¹¹Shall be told thy kindness in the grave?
Or in the abyss thy faithfulness?
¹²Shall thy wonders in the dark be known? And thy
righteousness in country of forgetfulness?

¹³But to thee I've cried, O Yahweh; and
in the morn my prayer shall come to thee.
¹⁴Why castest, Lord, thou off my soul?
Why hidest thou thy face from me?

·¹⁵I am wretched and prepared to die
upward from my youth: I'm mystified
while I bear thy terrors.¹⁶Over me thy fierce
wrath hath passed; thy terrors have me nullified.

¹⁷Came they round about me daily like
water; they together compassed me.
¹⁸Thou hast taken friend and lover far from me,
mine acquaintances into obscurity.

Psalm 89

I will sing for ever of
the mercies of the LORD: with my
mouth to generations all,
tell thy faithfulness will I.

²For I've stated, Edified
forever shall be steadfast love:
and thy faithfulness shalt thou
stablish in the heav'ns above.

·³With my chosen I have made a covenant,
I have sworn unto my servant David,⁴thy
seed I'll stablish evermore, and to
ages all thy throne I'll edify.   *Selah.*

⁵And thy wondrous miracles,
O LORD, the heavens shall confess:
yea, in the assembly of
holy ones, thy faithfulness.

⁶For in heaven who can be
compared to YAHWEH? Who can be
likened to the LORD among
children of a deity?

⁷In the council of the saints
is God to be intensely feared;
and of all them round about
him, he is to be revered.

·⁸YAHWEH God of hosts, who is a mighty LORD
like to thee? And round thee is thy faithfulness.
⁹Rulest thou the ocean's raging: when
rise its waves, thou makest them quiesce.

¹⁰Into pieces Rahab thou
hast broken, as one stricken dead;
with thy mighty arm, abroad
thou thine enemies hast spread.

¹¹Thine the heav'ns are, thine the earth
is also: thou hast set the base
of the world inhabited
and the fulness of that place.

¹²North and south thou hast created: Tabor and
Hermon shall with exultation sing in thy
name.¹³Thou hast a mighty arm: robust
is thy hand, and thy right hand is high.

¹⁴Righteousness and judgment are thy throne's support:
steadfast love and truth shall go in front of thy
face.¹⁵How blessèd are the people that
recognize the joyous festal cry:

in thy face's light, LORD, they
shall walk.¹⁶They shall rejoice all day
in thy name: and be upraised
in thy righteousness shall they.

¹⁷For thou art the glory of their strength: in thy
favor shall our horn exalted be as well.
¹⁸For the LORD is our defense; and our
king the Holy One of Israel.

¹⁹Then thou spakest in a vision unto thy
holy one, and saidst thou, Granted help have I
to one mighty; one that's chosen out
of the people I have lifted high.

²⁰I have found my servant David; with the oil
of my holiness, anointed him have I:
²¹one with whom my hand shall stablished be:
also shall mine arm him fortify.

²²Neither shall the enemy exact on him,
nor the son of wickedness him aggravate.
²³And before him I will beat his foes
down, and I will plague them that him hate.

²⁴But with him shall be my truth and mercy: and
in my name his horn shall be exalted.²⁵And
in the ocean I will set his hand,
in the rivers also his right hand.

²⁶Unto me shall he proclaim, My father art
thou, my God, and rock of my salvation.²⁷I
furthermore will make him my firstborn,
of the kings of earth the one most high.

[28] I will keep for him my mercy evermore,
and my covenant shall stand with him. [29] Always
will I also make his seed endure,
and his throne as long as heaven's days.

[30] If his sons forsake my law,
and in my judgments not proceed;
[31] if they break my statutes, and
my commands they fail to heed;

[32] then I'll visit their transgression with the rod,
and iniquity with lashes. [33] Nonetheless,
I'll not break my kindness off from him,
nor allow to fail my faithfulness.

[34] I will not profane my covenant, nor will
alter that which from my lips is uttered. [35] I
once have sworn upon my holiness
that I unto David will not lie.

[36] Ever shall his seed endure, his throne as long
as the sun before me, also. [37] It shall be
stablished as the moon for ever, and
as a faithful witness heavenly. *Selah.*

[38] But thou hast rejected and abhorred, thou hast
been irate with thine anointed one. [39] Disdained
hast thou thy manservant's covenant:
to the ground his crown thou hast profaned.

[40] Thou hast broken all of his enclosures down;
thou hast brought his forts to ruin. [41] All of the
passers by the way despoil him:
to his neighbors a reproach is he.

[42] Thou hast set his adversaries' right hand up;
thou hast given all his enemies delight.
[43] Thou hast turned the sharpness of his sword,
and hast not sustained him in the fight.

[44] Thou hast made his glory cease,
and to the ground his throne hast cast.
[45] Thou hast slashed his days of youth:
covered him with shame thou hast. *Selah.*

⁴⁶How long, LORD? Wilt thou for ever hide thyself?
Shall thy fury, like a fire, burn? ⁴⁷Recall
thou how short my time is: why hast thou
made in vain the sons of humans all?

⁴⁸Who's the man that liveth on,
and shall not see mortality?
From the power of the grave,
liberate his soul shall he?   *Selah.*

⁴⁹Where, Lord, are thy kindnesses
of old? To David thou didst swear
in thy truth. ⁵⁰The scorn of thy
servants, Lord, in mind do bear,

which I in my bosom take
from all the nationalities
manifold; ⁵¹with which reproached
have, O LORD, thine enemies;

wherewith they've reproached the steps
of thine anointed. ⁵²Blessèd be
YAHWEH for eternity.
Verily, and verily.

Book IV

Psalm 90

¹ O Lord, in generations all thou hast been our
abode. ²Before the mountains had their start,
or ever thou hadst formed the earth and world,
yea, from eon unto eon, God thou art.

³Thou turnest mortals into dust; and sayest thou,
Return, ye sons of men. ⁴For in thy sight
a thousand years are but as yesterday
when it's past, and as a watching in the night.

⁵Them thou carriest away
as with a flood; asleep are they:
in the morning they are like
the newly sprouting hay.

⁶It bloometh in the morning, and it groweth up;
and in the evening it is concised,
and withereth. ⁷For we're consumed by thine
anger, and we by thy wrath are terrorized.

⁸In front of thee hast set thou our iniquities,
and in thy face's light our sins concealed.
⁹For all our days are passed away in thy
wrath: our years expend we as a story spieled.

¹⁰The days of years of us are threescore years and ten;
and if by strength then fourscore years be they,
their strength is only toil and sorrow; for
soon it is curtailed, and we fly away.

¹¹Who fathometh the power of thine anger? And
according to the fear of thee is thy
displeasure. ¹²So us teach to count our days,
that we unto wisdom may our hearts apply.

¹³Return thou, O JϾHOVAH! How much longer? And
about thy servants let repent it thee.
¹⁴O sate us early with thy mercy; that
all our days we may rejoice and joyful be.

¹⁵Rejoice thou us according to the days that thou
hast humbled us, the years of evil we
have witnessed. ¹⁶Let thy work appear to thy
servants, and thy glory to their progeny.

¹⁷And let upon us be the beauty of the Lord
our God: and furthermore establish thou
the labor of our hands upon ourselves;
yea, the labor of our hands establish thou.

Psalm 91

¹ He that dwelleth in the covert of the One Supreme
in the shadow of th'Almighty shall abide.
²I will say of YAHWEH, He my refuge and
fortress is: my God; in him will I confide.

³Surely thee he shall deliver from the fowler's snare,
from the noisome pestilence. ⁴He'll cover thee
with his feathers, and beneath his wings shalt thou
trust, with shield and buckler his fidelity.

⁵Thou shalt not be frightened for the terror of the night;
neither for the arrow flying in the day;
⁶for the pestilence advancing in the dark;
for the ruin wasting at the noon of day.

⁷At thy side shall fall a thousand, and ten thousand at
thy right hand; but it shall not come nigh to thee.
⁸Only with thine eyes shalt thou consider, and
the reward of the ungodly thou shalt see.

⁹For, O LORD, thou art my refuge. Thou hast made
the One Supreme thy habitation;
¹⁰no evil shall befall thee, nor
approach thy dwelling shall contagion.

¹¹For he'll give his angels charge concerning thee, to keep
thee in all thy ways. ¹²They in their hands shall take
up thee, lest thou dash thy foot against a stone.
¹³Thou shalt tread upon the lion and the snake:

thou shalt trample underfoot the youthful lion and
dragon. ¹⁴Since upon me he hath set his love,
so will I deliver him: because he hath
known my name, I'll set him safely high above.

¹⁵He shall call on me, and I will answer him: I will
be with him in trouble; I will set him free,
and will honor him. ¹⁶With length of days I'll sate
him, and my salvation I will make him see.

Psalm 92

¹ It is good to thank JEHOVAH, and to sing
praises to thy name, O One Supreme: ² to tell
thy lovingkindness at the break of day,
ev'ry night thy faithfulness as well,

³ on the lute of ten strings, on the psaltery
also; on the harp with music resonant.
⁴ For through thy work, LORD, thou hast cheered me: I'll
in thy handiworks be jubilant.

⁵ O LORD, how great thy works are! And
thy thoughts exceedingly abstruse.
⁶ A brutish fellow knoweth not;
nor doth understand this one obtuse.

⁷ When the wicked flourish as the grass, and when
blossom all the workers of iniquity;
it's so they'll be destroyed for ever: ⁸ but
thou, LORD, art on high eternally.

⁹ For, lo, LORD, thy foes, for, lo, thy foes shall cease;
scattered shall be all who work iniquity.
¹⁰ But like an ox my horn shalt thou exalt:
bathed in verdant oil shall I be.

¹¹ Moreover my desire upon
mine enemies mine eye shall see;
mine ears as well shall hear my wish
of the wicked that arise on me.

¹² Flourish like the palm tree shall the righteous: grow
shall he like in Lebanon a cedar tree.
¹³ Those planted in JEHOVAH's house shall bloom
in the courtyards of our Deity.

¹⁴ Still in hoary-headed age shall bear they fruit;
fat and flourishing shall they be; ¹⁵ to confess
that upright is JEHOVAH: he's my rock,
and in him is no unrighteousness.

Psalm 93

· JEHOVAH reigneth, he is clothed with majesty;
JEHOVAH is attired with strength; himself hath girded he:

· indeed, the world is fixed, that moved it cannot be.
²Established is thy throne of old, thou from antiquity.

³The floods have lifted up,
O LORD, the inundations
have lifted up their voice;
the floods uplift their undulations.

· ⁴The LORD on high excelleth the cacophony
of many waters, yea, the mighty billows of the sea.

· ⁵Thy testimonies are assured exceedingly:
LORD, holiness is suited to thy house eternally.

Psalm 94

JEHOVAH God of vengeances;
God of vengeances, thyself do show.
²Lift thyself, thou judge of earth:
upon the proud reward bestow.

³O LORD, how long shall wicked ones,
how long shall the wicked gloat? ⁴Express
and declare they hubris. All
them boast that practice wickedness.

⁵In pieces break thy people they,
LORD, and they thy heritage oppress.
⁶Widow and sojourner they
dispatch; they slay the fatherless.

⁷Yet they say, JEHOVAH shall not notice, nor
shall the God of Jacob mark it. ⁸Ye
imbeciles among the people: understand;
and ye foolish, when will wise ye be?

⁹He that fastened on the ear, shall not he hear?
He that formed the eye, shall not he see?
¹⁰He that floggeth nations, shall he not correct?
He that teacheth mankind knowledge, he?

¹¹The LORD doth know the thoughts of man,
that they're vanity.¹²The man is bless'd
whom thou chastenest, O LORD,
whom from thy law thou tutorest;

¹³that from the days of evil thou
mayest give him rest, until the pit
for the villain's digged.¹⁴Because
the LORD will not his people quit,

he neither will abandon his
heirloom.¹⁵But return shall judgment to
righteousness: and all the ones
of upright heart shall it pursue.

¹⁶Who will arise for me against
those who practice evil? Who for me
will assume a stand against
the workers of iniquity?

¹⁷Unless the LORD had been my help,
   almost had my soul in silence dwelled.
¹⁸When I said, My foot doth slip;
   O LORD, thy mercy me upheld.

¹⁹In abundance of my thoughts within me, thy
   consolations soothe my soul. ²⁰With thee
   shall the throne of wickedness have fellowship,
   that which frameth mischief by decree?

²¹Gather they themselves as one against the soul
   of the righteous, and condemn they the
   guiltless blood. ²²JEHOVAH, though, is my defense;
   and my God the rock to which I flee.

²³And he shall bring upon them their
   own iniquity and cut them off
   in their own malignancy;
   the LORD our God shall cut them off.

Psalm 95

Come, unto JEHOVAH let us
sing in jubilance:
let us shout unto the rock of
our deliverance.

^{2}Let us with thanksgiving come before his face,
and make to him with psalms a joyful call.
^{3}For JEHOVAH is a great God,
and a great King above gods all.

^{4}In his hand are the recesses of the earth:
the strength of mountains his is furthermore.
^{5}His the sea is, and he made it:
and his hands formed the moistless shore.

^{6}Come, let's bow and worship: let us kneel before
the LORD our maker. ^{7}For our God is he;
and the people of his pasture
and the sheep of his hand are we.

If today ye hear his voice, ^{8}then harden not
your heart, as in the provocation, and
as the day of the temptation
in the uncultivated land:

^{9}when your fathers tried me, proved me,
and my work perceived.
^{10}Forty years long was I with this
generation grieved,

and I said, It is a people that do err
in heart; my ways have also known they not:
^{11}so I in my wrath did swear, They'll
not come into my resting spot.

Psalm 96

Sing unto the LORD an anthem new:
all the earth, unto JEHOVAH sing.
²Sing unto JEHOVAH, bless his name;
from day to day of his salvation tidings bring.

· ³Tell his glory in the nations, his
doings marvelous in all humanity.
⁴For the LORD is great, and greatly to be praised:
to be dreaded over all the gods is he.

· ⁵For the nations' deities are all
idols, but JEHOVAH made the firmament.
⁶Majesty and honor are before his face;
in his sanctuary, strength and ornament.

· ⁷Give unto the LORD, ye peoples' clans,
give unto the LORD prestige and potency.
⁸Give unto the LORD the glory due his name:
bring an off'ring, and his courtyards enter ye.

· ⁹Worship ye the LORD in ornament
holy: all the earth, before him tremble. ¹⁰Say
in the nations that JEHOVAH reigneth: yea,
stablished shall the world be that it shall not sway:

· he shall judge the people righteously.
¹¹Let rejoice the heavens, and the earth let spin
gladly; let the ocean and its fulness roar.
¹²Let the field be jubilant, and all therein:

· then before the LORD shall all the wood's
trees rejoice:¹³ for cometh he, for cometh he
for to judge the earth: with righteousness he shall
judge the world, and with his truth humanity.

Psalm 97

¹ Yahweh reigneth; let the earth rejoice;
let be jubilant the many isles.
²About him round are clouds and darkness: of his throne,
righteousness and judgment are the domicile.

³Fire before him goeth, and his
foes it burneth up around.
⁴Light the world up did his lightnings:
see and tremble did the ground.

⁵Hills at Yahweh's presence ran like wax,
at the presence of the Lord of all
the earth. ⁶The heavens demonstrate his righteousness,
and behold his glory do the people all.

⁷All of them that worship graven
images confounded be,
yea, that boast in idols: worship
him ye, ev'ry deity.

⁸Zion heard, and gladdened; and rejoiced
Judah's daughters on account, Lord, of
thy judgments. ⁹For thou, Lord, art high o'er all the earth:
all the gods thou art exalted far above.

¹⁰Yahweh's lovers, hate ye evil::
guardeth he his holy ones'
souls; them he delivereth out
of the hand of hooligans.

¹¹Light is planted for the righteous, and
gladness for the upright ones in heart.
¹²Rejoice, ye righteous, in the Lord; and gratitude
at remembrance of his holiness impart.

Psalm 98

Sing unto the LORD an anthem new;
for done amazing things hath he:
his right hand, and his arm of holiness,
hath secured for him the victory.

²The LORD hath rendered his salvation known:
in the sight of nations hath his righteousness he shown.

³Toward the house of Israel, he hath
recalled his lovingkindness and
his truth: beheld deliverance of our
God have all the limits of the land.

⁴A joyful noise unto JEHOVAH raise,
all the earth: a clamor make, rejoice, and sing ye praise.

⁵Sing unto JEHOVAH with the harp;
with harp and voice of psalm do sing.
⁶With trumpets and the sound of cornet make
joyful noise before the LORD, the King.

⁷Let the ocean and its fulness roar;
the world, and they that therein dwell.
⁸Let clap their hands the floods: before the LORD
let the hills for joy together yell;

⁹because to judge the earth he cometh: he
shall with justice judge the world, and clans with equity.

Psalm 99

Yahweh reigneth; let
the people tremble: he
sitteth on the cherubim;
moved the earth shall be.

²The Lord is great in Zion; and
he is high o'er all humanity.
³Let them praise thy great and terrible
name; for hallowèd is he.

⁴The power also of the king
loveth judgment; thou dost institute
equity; in Jacob, judgment and
justice thou dost execute.

⁵Lift ye up the Lord
our God, and worship ye
at the stool of his feet;
hallowèd is he.

⁶Among his priests were Moses and
Aaron, and among the ones that cry
out his name was Samuel. On the Lord
called they; gave he them reply.

⁷Within the cloudy pillar, he
spake to them: his testimonies they
kept, and they observed the ordinance
that to them he did convey.

⁸O Yahweh, God of us, thou them
answeredst: thou wast a pardoning
God to them, although thou didst exact
vengeance on their wrongdoings.

⁹Lift ye up the Lord
our God, and bow at his
holy mountain; for our God
Yahweh holy is.

Psalm 100

¹ Make a joyful noise unto the LORD,
all ye lands. ²With jubilance,
serve JEHOVAH: come with singing
ye before his countenance.

³Know ye that JEHOVAH he is God.
He hath made us; it is he
and not we ourselves. His people
and his pasture's sheep are we.

⁴With thanksgiving come into his
gates, his courtyards with acclaim:
unto him be thankful,
also bless his name.

⁵For the LORD is good; enduring
ever is his love steadfast;
and to generations
all, his truth doth last.

Psalm 101

- Of steadfast love and judgment I
  will sing: J{\sc ehovah}, unto thee
  will sing I. ²In a perfect way,
  will act I conscientiously.

- O when wilt thou come unto me?
  Within my house I will progress
  with perfect heart. ³Before mine eyes,
  will set I nothing valueless:

- I hate the work of them that turn
  aside; to me it shall not cling.
  ⁴A froward heart shall turn from me:
  I will not know a wicked being.

- ⁵Him who in secret slandereth
  his neighbor will I extirpate:
  the person high of look and proud
  of heart I will not tolerate.

- ⁶Mine eyes are on the faithful of
  the land, that they may dwell with me:
  the one that in a perfect way
  doth walk shall minister to me.

  ⁷Within my house the worker of
  deceit shall not reside:
  he that telleth lies shall not
  in my sight abide.

- ⁸The wicked of the land will I
  destroy in full at break of day,
  to from J{\sc ehovah}'s city cut
  the evildoers all away.

Psalm 102

¹ Lord, hear my prayer and unto thee let come my cry.
²In the day when I am in adversity,
from me conceal thy face not; bend thine ear to me:
in the day I call, me answer speedily.

³For passed like smoke my days are, and
my bones are burned as embers hot.
⁴My heart is smitten like the grass, and withered; so
that I, to eat my bread, remember not.

⁵By reason of my groaning's voice,
unto my skin my bones adhere.
⁶I'm like unto a pelican of wilderness:
I'm like a little owl of places sere.

⁷I watch, and as a sparrow, I
upon the housetop am forlorn.
⁸Mine enemies reproach me all the day; they that
are mad against me are against me sworn.

⁹For I have eaten ash like bread;
I've mixed my drink with tears also,
¹⁰by reason of thine indignation and thy wrath:
for thou hast raised me high, and cast me low.

¹¹My days are like a shadow that declineth; and
I, like grass, am withered.¹²But eternally
shalt thou, O Lord, continue on; and unto all
generations shall endure thy memory.

¹³Thou shalt arise, and shalt on Zion mercy have:
for the time to favor her, indeed, the time
appointed, is arrived.¹⁴Because thy servants take
pleasure in her stones, and they lament her grime.

¹⁵The heathen thus shall fear the name
of Yahweh, all the royalty
of earth thy glory also.¹⁶For the Lord shall build
up Zion; in his glory, show shall he.

¹⁷Regard will he the prayer of the forlorn, and not
scorn their prayer.¹⁸For generations yet to come
shall this be written: and a people which shall be
formed shall give unto the Lord encomium.

[19] For from the highness of his sanctuary hath
looked he down; from heav'n the LORD did contemplate
the earth; [20] to hear the groaning of the pris'ner; to
those appointed unto death emancipate;

[21] to tell in Zion YAHWEH's name,
and in Jerusalem relate
his praise; [22] when for to serve the LORD the people, and
the kingdoms, are together congregate.

[23] My strength he weakened in the way;
my days he docked. [24] I pleaded, Haul
me not away, my God, in middle of my days:
thy years endure through generations all.

[25] Of old hast laid thou the foundation of the earth;
and the heavens are thy hands' achievement. [26] They
themselves shall perish, but thou shalt endure: indeed,
like a garment all of them shall wear away;

as vesture shalt thou change them, and they shall be changed:
[27] but thou art the same, thy years shall never be
complete. [28] Thy servants' children shall abide, and their
seed shall be established in the sight of thee.

Psalm 103

Bless J‍EHOVAH, O my soul: and all
within me, bless his name of sanctity.
²Bless J‍EHOVAH, O my soul; forget thou not
all his dealings benefactory:

³who pardoneth all thine iniquities;
who maketh well from all thy maladies;
⁴who ransometh thy life from pit of hell;
who crowneth thee with steadfast love and sympathies;

⁵who satisfieth thy desire with good;
so like the eagle's is thy youth renewed.
⁶J‍EHOVAH executeth righteousness
and judgment unto all of them that are subdued.

⁷He made his courses known to Moses, and
his acts unto the sons of Israel.
⁸The L‍ORD is gracious and compassionate,
to anger slow, in mercy plenteous as well.

⁹He will not always chide: nor will he keep
his anger for eternity. ¹⁰With us,
he hath not dealt according to our sins;
nor as to our iniquities rewarded us.

¹¹For as the heav'n is high above the earth,
toward them that fear him great's his clemency.
¹²As far as east is from the west, so far
away from us hath taken our transgressions he.

¹³As a father hath compassion on
his children, so the L‍ORD hath sympathy
on the ones that fear him. ¹⁴For he knoweth our
frame; rememb'reth he that dust are we.

¹⁵But as for man, as grass his days are: as
a flow'r of field, so flourisheth he. ¹⁶For
the wind through it doth pass, and it is gone;
the place thereof shall not regard it anymore.

¹⁷But the mercy of the L‍ORD is from
eternity unto eternity
on the ones that fear him, and his righteousness
unto progeny of progeny;

¹⁸to the keepers of his covenant,
and to the people that in mem'ry bear
his commandments to perform them.¹⁹In the heav'ns,
hath the LORD prepared his royal chair;

and his kingdom ruleth over all.
²⁰O bless the LORD, his angels, that exceed
in robustness, ye that execute his word,
to his saying's voice according heed.

²¹Bless JEHOVAH, all his armies; ye
his ministers, that do his will divine.
²²Bless JEHOVAH, all his works in all his realm's
places: bless the LORD, O soul of mine.

Psalm 104

¹ O bless the Lord, my soul. O Lord my God, thou art
so great; thou art attired with pomp and majesty.
²Who coverest thyself with light as with a cloak:
who stretchest out the heavens like a drapery:

³who layeth rafters of his upper chambers in
the waters: who appointeth heavy clouds his chaise:
who walketh on the wings of wind:⁴who maketh winds
his messengers; his ministers a fire ablaze:

⁵who stablished the foundations of the earth,
that it forevermore should not be swayed.
⁶As with a garment, coveredst it thou
with the deep: above the hills the waters stayed.

⁷At thy rebuke they fled; at rumble of
thy thunder, ran away in fright they fast.
⁸They go up mountains; valleys they go down
to the place which thou for them established hast.

⁹A bound hast set thou, over which they may
not pass; so that to cover earth they no
more turn.¹⁰Into the valleys sendeth forth
he the fountains, which between the mountains flow.

¹¹To ev'ry creature of the field give
they drink: their thirst the asses wild allay.
¹²Beside them flyers of the heaven shall
have their dwelling; sing among the branches they.

¹³He watereth the mountains from his rooms: the earth
is sated with thy labors' fruit.¹⁴He maketh sprout
the grass for cattle, and the herb for use of man:
that from the earth may nourishment extract he out;

¹⁵and wine that maketh glad the heart of man, and oil
to make his face to shine, and bread which maketh strong
the heart of man.¹⁶Jehovah's trees are full of sap;
the cedars which hath planted he in Lebanon;

¹⁷wherein the birds construct their nests: as for the stork,
the fir trees are her house.¹⁸The mountains elevate
are refuge for the ibexes, as are the rocks
for conies.¹⁹For the times, the moon did he create:

the sun doth know his setting.[20] Darkness thou
imposest, and it's night: wherein do sneak
forth all forestial beasts.[21] The lion cubs
roar for prey, and they from God their meat do seek.

[22] The sun ariseth, gather they themselves
together, and within their dens they lay
them down.[23] Proceedeth man unto his work
and unto his labor till the close of day.

[24] O Lord, how manifold thy works are! Thou hast made
them all in wisdom: of thy wealth is satiate
the earth.[25] So is this ocean great and wide, wherein
are countless creepers, animals both small and great.

[26] There go the ships: there is leviathan,
whom thou hast made to play therein.[27] Await
these all upon thee; that thou mayest give
unto them their meat at time appropriate.

[28] Thou givest them, they gather it: thy hand
thou openest, with goodness filled are they.
[29] Thy face thou hidest, they are vexed: their breath
takest thou, they die, return they to their clay.

[30] Thou sendest forth thy spirit, they are formed:
the soil's surface thou dost renovate.
[31] The glory of Jehovah shall endure
alway: in his works the Lord shall jubilate.

[32] He looketh on the earth, and trembleth it:
he toucheth hills, and smoke they.[33] I will sing
unto the Lord as long as I'm alive:
praise I'll sing unto my God while I have being.

[34] To him my meditation shall be sweet: I will
be joyful in the Lord.[35] Consumed let sinners be
from off the earth, and let the wicked be no more.
O bless the Lord, my soul. Acclaim Jehovah ye!

Psalm 105

¹ O thank JEHOVAH; call upon his name:
declare his deeds among the populace.
² O sing to him ye, sing ye psalms to him:
commune on all his doings marvelous.

³ Glory in his holy name:
let rejoice the heart of them that seek
JEHOVAH. ⁴ Seek JEHOVAH, and
his strength: his face forever seek.

⁵ Recall his wondrous works that he hath done;
his signs and mouth's judicial renderings;
⁶ ye seed of Abraham his servant, ye
the sons of Jacob, ye his chosen beings.

⁷ The LORD our God is he: his judgments are
in all the earth. ⁸ He hath eternally
recalled his covenant, the word which to
a thousand generations ordered he.

⁹ Which covenant he made with Abraham,
his oath to Isaac, too; ¹⁰ confirmed as well
it he to Jacob for a law, and for
an endless covenant to Israel:

¹¹ declaring, Unto thee I'll give the land
of Canaan, lot of your inheritance:
¹² when they were but a few in number; yea,
a very few, and in it immigrants.

¹³ From nation to another nation, and
from kingdom to another realm they moved;
¹⁴ permitted he no man to do them wrong:
indeed, on their account he kings reproved:

¹⁵ commanding, Touch ye mine anointed not,
and to my prophets do no injury.
¹⁶ And he proclaimed a famine on the land:
he brake the staff of bread entirely.

¹⁷ He before them sent a man,
even Joseph, who to slavery
was sold: ¹⁸ whose feet with fetters they
afflicted: laid in iron was he:

^{19}until the time that came his word to pass:
Jehovah's saying tested him.^{20}The king
did send and loose him; yea, the ruler of
the people did, and free did he him spring.

^{21}Lord he made him of his house,
and the ruler of his riches' sum:
^{22}to bind his princes at his wish;
and teach his senators wisdom.

^{23}Israel to Egypt came
also; Jacob did indeed abide
within the land of Ham.^{24}And he
his people greatly multiplied;

and he made them mightier
than their foes.^{25}Their heart perverted he
to hate his people, to conspire
against his servants subtilely.

^{26}He sent his servant Moses; Aaron, too,
whom he had chosen for himself.^{27}Ordain
did he in them the matters of his signs
and of his miracles in Ham's terrain.

^{28}Sent he darkness, and he made
dark; and they rebelled against his word.
^{29}He turned their waters into blood;
their fish he also massacred.

^{30}Teemed their land with countless frogs,
in the chambers of their royalties.
^{31}He spake, and came there swarms of flies,
and lice in all their boundaries.

^{32}Gave he hail to them for rains,
flaming fire in their land.^{33}He thrashed
their vines and fig trees also; and
the arbors of their coasts he smashed.

^{34}He spake, and came there forth the locust and
the cankerworm, in number lacking bound,
^{35}and all the herbage in their land it ate,
and it devoured the produce of their ground.

^{36}And smote he all the firstborn in their land,
the chief of all their strength. ^{37}He also brought
them forth with gold and silver: and among
their tribes one feeble person there was not.

^{38}When they departed, Egypt was elate,
because the fear of them upon them fell.
^{39}He spread a cloud above for covering;
and fire to illume the night as well.

^{40}The people asked, and brought he quails, and he
with bread of heaven did them satisfy.
^{41}The rock he opened, and the waters gushed;
they ran, a river in the places dry.

^{42}For he recalled his holy promise, made
unto his servant Abraham. ^{43}And he
conveyed his people forth with gladness, and
his chosen persons with felicity:

^{44}and gave he them the heathen's lands: and they
inherited the people's industry;
^{45}in order that his statutes they might keep,
and guard his laws. Acclaim JEHOVAH ye.

Psalm 106

¹ Praise the L ORD. O give ye thanks unto the L ORD
for good: because his steadfast love always
endureth. ²Who can speak the mighty acts
of J EHOVAH? Who can publish all his praise?

³Blessed are the ones that care for judgment, he
that doeth righteousness in seasons all.
⁴Remember me, L ORD, with goodwill to thy
people: O with thy salvation, on me call;

⁵that I may behold thy chosen's
good, that in thy nation's jubilance
I may rejoice, in order that
I may boast with thine inheritance.

⁶We have sinned together with our
fathers, we iniquity have wrought,
we've wrongly done. ⁷Our fathers in
Egypt understood thy wonders not;

the abundance of thy mercies
they remembered not; but at the sea
provoked him, at the Sea of Reeds.
⁸For his name's account, though, saved them he,

so that he might make his mighty power to
be known. ⁹Moreover he did reprimand
the Sea of Reeds, and it was dried: so he
led them through the depths, as through the desert land.

¹⁰Also from the hand of him that hated them,
he saved them; furthermore, them he regained
from hand of foe. ¹¹The waters covered their
enemies as well: not one of them remained.

¹²Then believed they in his words; they sang his praise.
¹³They soon forgat his works; they did not bide
his counsel: ¹⁴but they in the wilderness
lusted much, and in the desert they God tried.

¹⁵And he gave them their request; but
sent a leanness in their soul. ¹⁶Inside
the camp, they envied Moses, and
Aaron, of J EHOVAH sanctified.

[17] Open did the earth and swallowed Dathan down,
and covered up Abiram's company.
[18] And in their company was kindled a
fire; the flame cremated persons ungodly.

[19] They produced a calf in Horeb,
and they bowed unto the molten. [20] They
thus changed their glory into the
likeness of an ox that eateth hay.

[21] They forgat their saviour God, which
had in Egypt done magnific deeds;
[22] amazements in the land of Ham,
things terrific by the Sea of Reeds.

[23] So he said he would destroy them,
if his chosen Moses had not stood
before him in the breach, to turn
back his fury, lest destroy he should.

[24] Yea, despised the pleasant land they,
in his promise they did not believe:
[25] but murmured they within their tents,
and JEHOVAH's voice did not perceive.

[26] Therefore he against them lifted up his hand,
to overthrow them in the desert sands:
[27] to overthrow their seed as well among
nations, and to scatter them throughout the lands.

[28] And they joined themselves to Baalpeor, and ate
the sacrifices of the lifeless folk.
[29] With their inventions they provoked him to
anger thus: the plague then in upon them broke.

[30] Then stood Phinehas, and executed he
atonement: and the plague was stayed. [31] And it
was counted unto him for righteousness
ever unto generations infinite.

[32] And they angered at the waters of dispute,
so ill it went with Moses for their sake:
[33] because his spirit they provoked, so that
with his lips he inconsiderately spake.

^{34}They did not destroy the nations,
which JEHOVAH did unto them say:
^{35}but they among the heathen were
intermixed, and learn their works did they.

^{36}Furthermore they served their idols:
which became a snare unto them. ^{37}Yea,
unto the devils sacrificed
their own sons and their own daughters they,

^{38}also shed they guiltless blood, indeed the blood
of their own sons and daughters, whom they slew
in sacrifice unto the idols of
Canaan: with the blood the land was sullied, too.

^{39}Thus were they defiled with their own works, and went
a whoring in their practices. ^{40}So burn
against his people did JEHOVAH's wrath,
insomuch that he his heritage did spurn.

^{41}And he gave them up into the heathen's hand;
and over them their haters governed. ^{42}And
their enemies oppressed them, and they were
into subjugation brought beneath their hand.

^{43}Oft he rescued them; but they provoked him with
their counsel, and for their iniquity
were brought they low. ^{44}He looked on their distress
nonetheless, when heard their lamentation he:

^{45}and remembered he for them his covenant,
and in abundance of his clemencies
repented. ^{46}Of those all that carried them
captives, also gave he them to sympathies.

^{47}Save thou us, O LORD our God, and
from the infidels us congregate,
to give unto thy holy name
thanks and, in thy praise, to celebrate.

^{48}Blessed may JEHOVAH, God of
Israel, be from eternity
unto eternity: let all
people say, Amen. Acclaim JAH ye.

Book V

Psalm 107

¹ Give ye thanks unto J‍ehovah, for he's good:
for his mercy lasteth for eternity.
² Let so say the ransomed of J‍ehovah, whom
from the adversary's hand hath ransomed he;

³ and them he assembled from the countries, from
east and west, from north and south. ⁴ Meandered they
in the desert in a solitary way;
found they not a settlement in which to stay.

⁵ Hungry also thirsty, swooned their soul
in them. ⁶ Then in their trouble they
cried unto J‍ehovah, and from their
distresses them he snatched away.

⁷ And he led them forth in level way, that they
might unto a town of habitation go.
⁸ Oh that for his goodness men would praise the L‍ord,
for his wondrous works to sons of men also!

⁹ For he satisfieth the desirous soul,
and with goodness he the hungry soul doth fill.
¹⁰ Such as sit in darkness and the shadow of
death: in hardship and in iron shackled still;

¹¹ on account that they rebelled against God's words,
and contemned the counsel of the Highest One:
¹² so with grievous labor, brought he down their heart;
fell they down, and there to render help was none.

¹³ Then they in their trouble cried unto the L‍ord,
and them he delivered from their tight constraints.
¹⁴ Brought he them from darkness and the shadow of
death, he also brake in sunder their restraints.

¹⁵ Oh that for his goodness men would praise the L‍ord,
and for his extraordinary works unto
sons of men! ¹⁶ For he hath smashed the gates of brass,
and the bars of iron hath he cut in two.

¹⁷ Fools are afflicted on account of their
trespass, and because of their iniquities.
¹⁸ Ev'ry kind of meat abominateth their
soul; and near unto the gates of death they ease.

¹⁹And they in their trouble cry unto
JEHOVAH, them he then doth save
from their straits.²⁰He sent his word, and them
he healed and rescued from their graves.

²¹Oh that for his goodness men would praise the LORD,
for his wondrous works to sons of men as well!
²²Let them sacrifice the sacrifices of
giving thanks, and with delight his doings tell.

²³Goers down into the sea in ships,
that earn in waters great their keep;
²⁴these behold the doings of the LORD,
his wonders also in the deep.

²⁵For commandeth he, and raiseth up
the stormy wind, which lifteth tall
waves thereof.²⁶They mount up to the heav'n,
again down to the depths they fall:

on account of jeopardy their soul
is melted.²⁷Reel they to and fro,
and they stagger like a drunken man,
their wits are swallowed up also.

²⁸Then they cry unto the LORD in their
distress, and from their troubles he
bringeth them.²⁹He maketh calm the storm
and stilleth billows of the sea.

³⁰Then they're glad because they're quiet; so them he
bringeth to the haven of their pleasure.³¹Oh
that they'd praise JEHOVAH for his goodness, and
for his wondrous works to sons of men also!

³²Also in the congregation of
the people, up let him them raise,
furthermore in the assembly of
the senators, let them him praise.

³³Turneth he the rivers into wilderness,
springs of water into thirsty ground as well;
³⁴fruitful land into a salty waste, because
of the wickedness of them that therein dwell.

^{35}Turneth he the desert into waterpools,
and the arid land to watersprings. ^{36}And there
maketh he the hungry to abide, that a
city for inhabitance they may prepare;

^{37}and may sow the fields, and vineyards plant, which may
yield fruits of increase. ^{38}And he doth them bless,
so that they are multiplied exceedingly;
and he letteth not their cattle number less.

^{39}Through oppression, evil, and unhappiness,
minished and prostrated once again are they.
^{40}Poureth he contempt on princes, causing them
to meander in the wilderness, not way.

^{41}Yet on high the poor he setteth from
affliction, and doth situate
families like a flock. ^{42}The righteous shall
behold it, and shall jubilate:

all iniquity shall stop her mouth.
^{43}Whoever's wise, and will attend
to these things, the lovingkindness of
JEHOVAH they shall apprehend.

Psalm 108

God, my heart is steadfast; I will sing
and strum, yea, with my glory. [2]Wake,
psaltery and harp: myself,
I will wake at morning's break.

· [3]I will praise thee, LORD, among the people: and
in the nations sing to thee will I.
[4]For above the heavens is thy mercy great:
and thy truth extendeth to the sky.

· [5]Be exalted, God, above the heavens; let
over all the earth thy glory be;
[6]that may be delivered thy belovèd: save
thou with thy right hand, and answer me.

· [7]God hath spoken in his sanctuary; I
will be joyful, Shechem I'll assign,
and will measure out the valley of Succoth.
[8]Gilead is mine; Manasseh's mine;

· and the helmet of my head is Ephraim;
Judah's my lawgiver; [9]Moab's my
washpot; over Edom will I cast my shoe;
triumph o'er Philistia will I.

· [10]Who will escort me into the fortified
city? Into Edom who'll me lead?
[11]Wilt not thou, God, who hast cast us off? And God,
with our hosts wilt not thou forth proceed?

[12]Give us help from trouble: for the help
of man is vain. [13]Through God shall we
bravely do: for he that shall
trample down our foes is he.

Psalm 109

Hold thy peace not, God of my
praise;² for opened wide on me
are the mouth of wickedness
and the mouth of treachery:

with a lying tongue, against me they have
spoken.³ They encompassed me about
with words of animosity as well;
and they fought against me, though a cause without.

⁴For my love they are mine adversaries:
but I give myself to prayer.⁵ And me
have they for good rewarded evil, and
for my love have given animosity.

⁶Set a wicked man above him: and let
Satan stand upon his right hand.⁷ When
he shall be judged, let him proceed declared
guilty: also let his prayer become as sin.

⁸Let his days be few; let some
other take his custody.
⁹Let his sons be fatherless,
and his wife a widow be.

¹⁰Let his children always be
vagabonds, and mendicate:
let them also seek their bread
from their places desolate.

¹¹Let the lender tangle all he hath; and
let the strangers spoil his industry.
¹²Let none extend compassion unto him:
nor let any show his orphans sympathy.

¹³Let his progeny be for
cutting off; as well in the
generation following,
let their name deleted be.

¹⁴Let his fathers' wickedness
with the LORD to mind be brought;
also let the sin of his
mother be deleted not.

¹⁵Let continually them
be before the LORD, that he
may of them eradicate
from the earth the memory.

¹⁶Forasmuch as he remembered not to
render mercy, but did persecute
the humble and the needy man, that the
brokenhearted he might even execute.

¹⁷As he cherished cursing, so
let it come to him: as he
took no joy in blessing, so
let it from him distant be.

¹⁸As he put on cursing like
as his garment, let it so
come like water in his bowels,
in his bones like oil also.

¹⁹As the cloak which covereth
him, let it unto him be,
also for a belt wherewith
he is girded constantly.

²⁰From the LORD, let this be mine
adversaries' recompense,
and of persons that on my
soul pronounce malevolence.

²¹But do thou for me, O Lord JEHOVAH,
for thy name's account: deliver me
for good thy mercy is. ²²For I am poor
and in need, and wounded is my heart in me.

²³Like the shadow when it doth decline, I'm
vanished: as the locust, high and low
I'm tossed. ²⁴Through fasting, feeble are my knees;
groweth lean my flesh for want of fat also.

²⁵Also a reproach to them became I:
shook their heads they when they looked on me.
²⁶Assist me, O my God JEHOVAH, and
save thou me according to thy clemency:

²⁷that they'll know that this thy hand is; that thou,
Lord, hast done it. ²⁸They shall execrate,
but thou shalt bless: when they arise, let them
be ashamed; but let thy servant jubilate.

²⁹Let mine adversaries be
clothed with shame, and let them drape
with their own confusion their
selves, as with an outer cape.

³⁰With my mouth, I'll greatly praise the Lord; yea,
in the multitude I'll him extol.
³¹For at the right hand of the poor shall he
stand, to save him from the ones that judge his soul.

Psalm 110

¹ Jehovah said unto my Lord, Upon my right
hand sit, until I make thy foes a stool
for thy feet. ²The Lord shall out of Zion send the rod
of thy strength: in middle of thy foes do rule.

³Thy people shall be willing in the day
of thy power, in resplendency
holy from the matrix of the morning: thou
hast the mist nocturnal of thy juvenility.

⁴The Lord hath sworn, and he will not repent,
Thou art priest for ever after the
order of Melchizedek. ⁵The Lord at thy
right hand, in his anger's day, shall strike through royalty.

⁶Among the heathen he shall judge, the places he
shall fill with lifeless bodies; he shall smite
heads of many countries. ⁷Of the river in the way
he shall drink: he thus shall lift the head to height.

Psalm 111

¹ Praise the L<small>ORD</small> ye! I will praise the L<small>ORD</small> with whole
heart, in the assembly of the persons right,
and the congregation. ²Doings of the L<small>ORD</small>
are great, they're sought by all that take therein delight.

³Glorious and splendid is his work; and his
righteousness endureth for eternity.
⁴He hath made his wondrous works to be recalled:
the L<small>ORD</small> is gracious and is full of clemency.

⁵He hath given meat to them that fear him: he
ever mindful of his covenant will be.
⁶He hath showed his people power of his works,
that give to them the heathen's heritage may he.

⁷His handiworks are truth and judgment; of
his commandments, all are trustworthy.
⁸Stand they fast for ever always,
done in truth and probity.

⁹He sent redemption to his people: his
covenant for time without an end
hath commanded he: his name is
hallowèd and reverend.

¹⁰The fear of Y<small>AHWEH</small>'s the beginning of
wisdom: good discernment have all they
that adhere to his commands: his
praise endureth for alway.

Psalm 112

· Acclaim J<small>EHOVAH</small>! Blessèd is the man
that doth fear the L<small>ORD</small>; delighteth greatly he
in his commandments. ²Strong shall be his seed on earth:
the generation of the upright bless'd shall be.

· ³Within his house shall wealth and riches be:
and his righteousness endureth ever. ⁴To
the upright, light ariseth in the darkness: he
is gracious, and compassionate, and righteous, too.

· ⁵A good man showeth grace, and lendeth: he
will conduct his matters with discretion. ⁶He
assuredly shall not be moved for evermore:
forever in remembrance shall the righteous be.

· ⁷Of evil tidings shan't he be afraid:
fixed his heart is, in J<small>EHOVAH</small> placing trust.
⁸Established is his heart, he shall not be afraid,
until upon his enemies he see his lust.

⁹Dispersed and given to the poor hath he;
his righteousness endureth endlessly;
with honor shall his horn exalted be.

¹⁰The wicked one shall see, and grievèd be;
then gnash his teeth and melt away shall he:
the villains' wish shall perish utterly.

Psalm 113

Praise JEHOVAH. Praise, ye servants
of the LORD, the name JEHOVAH praise.
²The name JEHOVAH shall be bless'd
from this time and for always.

³From the rising of the sun to its
setting, praised the name JEHOVAH is to be.
⁴The LORD is high above all nations,
and above the heavens is his majesty.

⁵Who is like the LORD our God, who
is enthroned on high, ⁶who, to attend
to matters in the heavens and
in the earth, doth condescend!

⁷From the dust the poor he raiseth up,
lifteth he from dunghill the necessitous;
⁸that he may make him sit with princes,
even with the princes of his populace.

⁹Maketh he the barren woman
to abide at home, to also be
a merryhearted mother of
children. Praise JEHOVAH ye!

Psalm 114

[1] When Israel departed Egypt, Jacob's house
from a people of a foreign lexicon;
[2] Judah was his sanctuary, and
Israel his dominion.

[3] The sea beheld it, and he fled:
back was Jordan rotated.

[4] The lofty mountains skipped like rams,
and the little hills like lambs.

[5] What agitated thee, thou sea, that fleddest thou?
That, thou Jordan, thou wast driven to retreat?
[6] O ye mountains, that ye skipped like rams;
and like lambs, ye hills petite?

[7] O earth, travail thou at the presence of the Lord,
at the countenance of Jacob's God, [8] the being
which converted rock to waterpool,
even flint to waterspring.

Psalm 115

· Not to us, Lord, not to us, but to thy name
give thou glory, for thy clemency,
and for thy truth's account,² lest nations should
question, Where is now their Deity?

·³But our God is in the heavens: he hath done
all of that to which he hath inclined.
⁴Their images are gold and silver, they
are the work of hands of humankind.

⁵They have mouth, but speak they not:
eyes have they, but see they not:
⁶they have ears, but hear they not:
nose have they, but smell they not:
⁷they have hands, but feel they not:
feet have they, but walk they not:

neither speak they through their throat.
⁸Unto them, they that them make
are akin; so's ev'ry one
that in them doth refuge take.

⁹Israel, in YAHWEH trust:
he's their helper and their shield.
¹⁰Aaron's house, in YAHWEH trust:
he's their helper and their shield.
¹¹YAHWEH's fear'rs, in YAHWEH trust:
he's their helper and their shield.

¹²Mindful of us hath the LORD
been: us he will bless; will bless
he the house of Israel;
he'll the house of Aaron bless.

¹³Them that fear the LORD he'll bless,
minor ones with major ones.
¹⁴More and more the LORD shall add
unto you, you and your sons.

·¹⁵Ye are blessèd of the LORD, which made the heav'n
and the earth.¹⁶The heaven, verily
the heavens, are the LORD's: but unto the
sons of men, the earth hath given he.

[17]Lifeless ones do not acclaim the LORD, nor all them that down to silence go. [18]But we will bless JEHOVAH from henceforth and for evermore. Acclaim JEHOVAH ye.

Psalm 116

¹ I love the LORD, because my voice and mine appeals hath he
heard. ²Because he hath inclined his ear to me,

therefore I will call upon him while
I live. ³The throes of death did me surround,
and the pains of hell gat hold on me:
affliction and distress I found.

⁴Then I called upon JEHOVAH's name;
deliver, LORD, my soul, with thee I plead.
⁵Gracious is the LORD, and righteous, too;
our God is merciful, indeed.

⁶Guard the simple doth the LORD: I was
enfeebled, and he helped me. ⁷To thy rest,
O my soul, return because the LORD
hath bountifully thee redressed.

⁸For thou hast removed my soul from death,
mine eyes from tears, my feet from stumblings.
⁹In the presence of JEHOVAH, I
will walk in lands of living beings.

¹⁰Believed I, thus I've spoken: I was greatly humbled. ¹¹I
said in mine alarum, Ev'ry man doth lie.

¹²What shall give I in requital to
JEHOVAH for his benefactions all
me toward? ¹³I'll take salvation's cup,
and on JEHOVAH's name I'll call.

¹⁴I will pay my vows unto the LORD
in front of all his people presently.
¹⁵Precious in JEHOVAH's vision is
his holy ones' mortality.

¹⁶O LORD, I truly am thy servant; I'm thy servant, and
son of thy handmaiden: thou hast loosed my bands.

¹⁷Sacrifice of thanks will offer I
to thee, and on JEHOVAH's name I'll call.
¹⁸Presently unto the LORD I'll pay
my vows before his people all,

[19] within the courtyards of Jehovah's house, in midst of thee,
O Jerusalem. Acclaim Jehovah ye.

Psalm 117

O praise the Lord, ye nations all:
praise him, all ye people. ²For his mercy toward
us is great: and Yahweh's truth
endureth evermore. Acclaim the Lord!

Psalm 118

Give ye thanks unto the Lord for good:
for his mercy lasteth evermore.
²Presently let Israel declare,
that his mercy lasteth evermore.

³Let the house of Aaron now declare,
that his mercy lasteth evermore.
⁴Let Jehovah's fearers now declare,
that his mercy lasteth evermore.

⁵Called I on Jehovah in distress:
unto me Jehovah gave reply;
me he set in open space. ⁶The Lord
is for me; afraid will not be I:

what can man do unto me? ⁷The Lord
is for me as one who helpeth me:
consequently my desire upon
them that hate me shall I come to see.

⁸Better 'tis to shelter in the Lord
than rely upon humanity.
⁹Better 'tis to shelter in the Lord
than rely upon nobility.

¹⁰All the nations compassed me about:
I will nonetheless demolish them
in Jehovah's name. ¹¹They compassed me
round about; yea, in did they me hem:

but I'll, in Jehovah's name, destroy
them. ¹²Like bees they compassed me about;
as the fire of thorns, they're quenched: because
in Jehovah's name, I'll wipe them out.

¹³Thou hast pushed me sore that I might fall:
but the Lord provided help to me.
¹⁴Jah's my strength and melody, and he
my deliverance is come to be.

¹⁵In the tabernacles of the ones
righteous is the voice of gladness and
of deliverance: courageously
doeth of Jehovah the right hand.

ⁱ⁶Lifted high's the right hand of the Lord:
doeth valiantly the Lord's hand right.
¹⁷I shan't die, but I shall live, and the
doings of the Lord shall I recite.

¹⁸Me the Lord hath chastened sore: but he
hath not unto death me given.¹⁹Throw
open ye the gates of righteousness
unto me: I into them will go,

and I'll praise the Lord:²⁰Jehovah's gate
this, in which the righteous ones shall come.
²¹I will praise thee: for thou hast me heard,
and art my deliverance become.

²²Stone the builders disallowed is the
head stone of the corner now become.
²³This is by the doing of the Lord;
in the eyes of us it's wondersome.

²⁴This the day is which the Lord hath made;
we'll rejoice and glad in it we'll be.
²⁵Save thou now, I beg thee, Lord: I, Lord,
beg thee, send thou now prosperity.

²⁶Bless'd be he that cometh in the name
of the Lord: we've bless'd you from the Lord's
house.²⁷The Lord is God and he hath showed us light:
to the altar's horns, secure the sacrifice with cords.

²⁸Thou my God art, and acclaim thee will
I: my God, and I will lift up thee.
²⁹Give ye thanks unto the Lord for good:
for his mercy's for eternity.

Psalm 119

ALEPH

¹ Blessed are the perfect in the way,
who in the law of Y<small>AHWEH</small> stride.
²Blessed are the ones that keep his testimonies,
that with all the heart him seek beside.

³They indeed do no iniquity:
they in his ways proceed.
⁴Thy precepts hast commanded thou
for us to diligently heed.

⁵O that to observe thy statutes may
directed be my ways!
⁶Ashamed I then shall not be, when
to thy commandments all I gaze.

⁷I, with uprightness of heart, will praise
thee, when thy judgments right
I shall have learned. ⁸I will observe
thy statutes: me forsake not quite.

BETH

⁹Wherewithal a lad shall cleanse his way?
By taking heed as to thy word. ¹⁰I've sought
thee with all my heart: from thy
commandments let me wander not.

¹¹Thy word have I hid in my heart,
that I might not sin against thee.
¹²Thou, JEHOVAH, blessèd art:
teach thy statutes unto me.

¹³With my lips have I recounted all
the judgments of thy mouth. ¹⁴I've taken glee
in thy testimonies's way,
as over all of luxury.

¹⁵In thy precepts I will meditate,
and have respect unto thy ways. ¹⁶In thy
ordinances I'll delight
myself: forget thy word won't I.

GIMEL

¹⁷With thy servant bountifully deal;
I may live then, and thy word preserve.
¹⁸Open thou mine eyes, that marvelous
matters from thy law I may observe.

¹⁹I am a sojourner in the earth:
hide thou thy commandments not from me.
²⁰Shattered is my soul with yen for thy
judgments that in seasons all hath she.

²¹Thou hast chided proud ones, cursèd ones
which from thy commandments go awry.
²²Roll from me reproach and disrespect;
for have kept thy testimonies I.

²³Princes sat and spoke against me: but
in thy statutes mused thy servant.²⁴Thy
testimonies, too, are my delight:
men who unto me advice supply.

DALETH

²⁵To the dust my soul doth cleave:
  according to thy word enliven me.
²⁶My ways have I declared, and thou
  me heardest: teach thy statutes unto me.

²⁷Make me understand thy precepts' way:
  talk then of thy wondrous works shall I.
²⁸On account of heaviness my soul doth melt:
  according to thy word me fortify.

²⁹Take from me the way of lies:
  and graciously provide thy law to me.
³⁰The way of truth have chosen I:
  thy judgments have I laid in front of me.

³¹To thy testimonies I
  have stuck: O put me not, Lord, to disgrace.
³²Because thou shalt enlarge my heart,
  the way of thy commandments I will race.

HE

³³ Teach thou me, O LORD, the way of thy
statutes; and I shall preserve it to the end.
³⁴ Make me understand, and I shall keep thy law;
yea, with all my heart it I shall tend.

³⁵ In the path of thy commandments make
me to go; for I therein delight.
³⁶ To thy testimonies bend my
heart, and not to gain unright.

³⁷ From beholding falsehood, turn thou mine
eyes away; and in thy way enliven me.
³⁸ Stablish thou thy word unto thy servant, who
is devoted to the fear of thee.

³⁹ Turn away my scorn, the which I fear:
for thy judgments they are good. ⁴⁰ Lo, I've
hankered for thy precepts: in thy
righteousness make me alive.

VAU

⁴¹ Let thy lovingmercies also come to me, LORD, yea,
  thy salvation, as unto thy word.
⁴² So I'll have wherewithal to answer him
  that reproacheth me: for trust I in thy word.

⁴³ And take not greatly from my mouth the word of truth;
  for I have hoped upon thy judgments. ⁴⁴ Thus
  I shall keep thy law continually
  ever without terminus.

⁴⁵ And I will walk at liberty because I seek
  thy precepts. ⁴⁶ Also I will speak of thy
  testimonies in the sight of kings,
  and ashamed will not be I.

⁴⁷ And delight myself will I in thy commandments, which
  I have loved. ⁴⁸ And I will elevate
  my hands to thy commandments, which I've loved;
  and upon thy statutes I will meditate.

ZAIN

⁴⁹Remember thou the word unto thy servant,
upon which thou hast given hope to me.
⁵⁰In mine affliction this is my
comfort: for thy word hath quickened me.

⁵¹The proud have had me greatly in derision:
yet from thy law have not I turned awry.
⁵²Thine ancient judgments I recalled,
Lord; and comforted myself have I.

⁵³Because of wicked people that abandon
thy law, hath horror taken hold of me.
⁵⁴Thy statutes have become my songs
in the dwelling of mine odyssey.

⁵⁵Thy name have I remembered, Lord,
in the night, and thy
law I've kept. ⁵⁶This came to me,
for kept thy precepts I.

CHETH

⁵⁷ LORD, thou art my portion: I have said that I
would keep thy words. ⁵⁸ With all my heart, conjured
I thy grace: be merciful unto
me according to thy word.

⁵⁹ On my ways I thought, and unto thy
testimonies turned my feet I back.
⁶⁰ Thy commandments hastened I
to keep, and I was none too slack.

⁶¹ Bands of wicked men have robbed me: I have not
forgotten, though, thy law. ⁶² At noon of night,
I will rise to offer thanks to thee
owing to thy judgments right.

⁶³ I am one conjoined to all them that thee fear,
and to the ones that keep thy precepts. ⁶⁴ The
earth, O LORD, is of thy mercy full:
teach thy statutes unto me.

TETH

^{65}According to thy word, LORD, well hast dealt
thou with thy servant. ^{66}Good discretion and
knowledge teach thou me: for I
have believed in thy commands.

^{67}Before I was distressed I went astray:
but I have kept thy saying presently.
^{68}Thou art good, and doest good;
teach thy statutes unto me.

^{69}The proud have forged a lie against me: but
thy precepts I will keep with all of my
heart. ^{70}Their heart's as fat as grease;
in thy law take pleasure I.

^{71}It is good for me that I have been distressed;
that I might learn thy statutory bounds.
^{72}Better is to me the law of thy
mouth above a thousand gold and silver rounds.

JOD

⁷³Thy hands have made me and have fashioned me:
provide me understanding; I shall learn then thy
commandments. ⁷⁴They that fear thee will be glad when they
behold me; for upon thy word have waited I.

⁷⁵I know, O Lord, that right thy judgments are,
and that in faithfulness thou hast afflicted me.
⁷⁶I pray thee, let thy kindness for my comfort be,
according to thy word unto the slave of thee.

⁷⁷Let come thy mercies unto me, that I
may live: because thy law is my delight. ⁷⁸Confused
shall be the proud; for they perversely dealt with me
without a cause: but in thy precepts I will muse.

⁷⁹Let those that fear thee unto me return,
and the persons that have known of thy
testimonies. ⁸⁰Let my heart be sound
in thy statutes; that ashamed may not be I.

CAPH

⁸¹My soul doth faint for thy salvation:
but upon thy word I wait.
⁸²For thy word mine eyes consume,
saying, When wilt thou me consolate?

⁸³For like a bottle in the smoke am I
become; thy statutes yet I do
not forget. ⁸⁴How many are thy servant's days? When wilt
thou bring judgment on the ones that me pursue?

⁸⁵The proud, which follow not thy law, have
excavated pits for me.
⁸⁶Thy commandments all are sure:
they pursue me wrongly; help thou me.

⁸⁷They almost had consumed me in the earth;
I nonetheless forsook not thy
precepts. ⁸⁸Quicken me according to thy kindness; so
keep the testimony of thy mouth shall I.

LAMED

⁸⁹JEHOVAH, for eternity thy word is fixed
securely in the heavens. ⁹⁰Thy fidelity
is unto ages all: the earth thou hast
established, and abideth she.

⁹¹According to thine ordinances, they this day
continue: for thy servants are the whole. ⁹²Unless
thy law had been my pleasures, I should then
have perished in my wretchedness.

⁹³I never will forget thy precepts: for
with them hast thou made me alive.
⁹⁴I am thine, deliver me;
for sought thy precepts I've.

⁹⁵The wicked ones have waited for me to destroy
me: but thy testimonies I will understand.
⁹⁶I've seen an end of all perfection: but
exceeding broad is thy command.

MEM

^{97}O how I love thy law! It's my
meditation the entire day.
^{98}Thou through thy commandments hast me made
wiser than my foes: for they're with me alway.

^{99}Perceive I more than all of my
teachers: for thy testimonies my
meditation are. ^{100}I understand
more than ancients, for preserve thy precepts I.

^{101}From ev'ry evil way I have refrained
my feet, that I might keep thy word. ^{102}I've not
departed from thy judgments:
for me thou hast taught.

^{103}How sweet thy words are to my taste!
Sweeter to my mouth than honey! ^{104}Through
thy commandments, understanding I
gather: therefore hate I ev'ry way untrue.

NUN

¹⁰⁵Thy word is a lamp unto my feet,
and unto my path a light.
¹⁰⁶I have sworn, I also will confirm,
that I will keep thy judgments right.

¹⁰⁷I'm very much afflicted: quicken me,
O Lord, according to thy word. ¹⁰⁸Beseech I thee,
accept the freewill off'rings of my mouth,
O Lord, and teach thy judgments unto me.

¹⁰⁹My soul's in my hand continually:
yet thy law I don't forget.
¹¹⁰Wicked ones have laid a snare for me:
I erred not from thy precepts yet.

¹¹¹Thy testimonies I've inherited
forevermore: for they're my heart's felicity.
¹¹²I have inclined my heart to execute
thy statutes alway, unto expiry.

SAMECH

[113] I hate the double-minded: but
thy law I love. [114] Thou my
hiding place and shield art:
tarry for thy word do I.

[115] Depart from me, ye evildoers: for I will
preserve my God's commands. [116] Uphold thou me
as unto thy word, that I may live:
also of my hope let me ashamed not be.

[117] Sustain me, and I shall be safe: and I will have
respect unto thy statutes constantly.
[118] Thou hast trodden all them down that err
from thy statutes: for their fraud is falsity.

[119] Thou trashest all the wicked of the earth like dross:
I therefore love thy testimonies. [120] My
flesh doth tremble for the fear of thee;
of thy judgments, furthermore, afraid am I.

AIN

[121] I have executed judgment and
justice: leave me not to mine oppressors. [122] Be
for thy servant surety for good:
let the proud oppress not me.

[123] Mine eyes fail for thy salvation, and
for the promise of thy righteousness. [124] As to
thy compassion, with thy servant deal;
teach thou me thy statutes, too.

[125] I'm thy servant; understanding give
me, in order that thy testimonies may
know I. [126] LORD, it's time for thee to work:
for thy law have broken they.

[127] Therefore thy commands I love above
gold; indeed, above fine gold. [128] I therefore rate
all thy precepts touching all as right;
ev'ry way untrue I hate.

PE

^{129}Wonderful thy testimonies are:
consequently doth my soul preserve them. ^{130}The
entrance of thy words enlighteneth;
it giveth to the simpletons sagacity.

^{131}Opened I my mouth, and panted: for
longed I after thy commandments. ^{132}Look unto
me, and mercy show to me, as to
the ones that love thy name is usual to do.

^{133}Order in thy word my footsteps: and
over me let no iniquity have reign.
^{134}From the plundering of humankind,
deliver me: thy precepts I will then maintain.

^{135}Make thy face to shine upon thy servant;
teach thy statutes unto me also.
^{136}Because they do not keep thy law,
down mine eyes do streams of waters flow.

TZADDI

¹³⁷ LORD, thou art righteous and thy judgments are
right. ¹³⁸ Thy testimonies that thou hast
commanded are in righteousness,
and exceedingly steadfast.

¹³⁹ My zeal hath consumed me, for thy words
have mine enemies forgotten. ¹⁴⁰ Pure
exceedingly thy word is: thy
servant therefore loveth her.

¹⁴¹ I'm small and one despised: thy precepts yet
I do not forget. ¹⁴² Eternally
thy righteousness is righteousness,
and thy law is verity.

¹⁴³ Trouble and distress have taken hold on me:
yet thy commandments are my pleasures. ¹⁴⁴ Thy
testimonies' righteousness is everlasting:
make me understand, and live shall I.

KOPH

¹⁴⁵I cried with all my heart; O Lord, me hear:
thy statutes I will keep.
¹⁴⁶Unto thee I cried; me save, and thy
testimonies I shall keep.

¹⁴⁷I rose before the dawn of morn, and cried:
I waited on thy word.
¹⁴⁸Mine eyes wake before the watches, that
I might ponder in thy word.

¹⁴⁹Hear my voice according to thy mercy: Lord,
quicken me according to thy judgment. ¹⁵⁰Draw
nigh do they that follow after mischief:
they are distant from thy law.

¹⁵¹Lord, thou art near; and thy commandments all
are truth. ¹⁵²I've known from yore
of thy testimonies that thou hast
founded them for evermore.

RESH

^{153}Look on mine affliction, and deliver me:
for thy law I've not forgotten. ^{154}Strive
for my cause, and me redeem:
as to thy saying, me revive.

^{155}From the wicked is salvation far: for they
do not seek thy statutes. ^{156}Great are thy
tender mercies, LORD: as to
thy judgments, me revivify.

^{157}My persecutors and my foes are numerous;
and yet I from thy testimonies do not swerve.
^{158}Beheld I the transgressors, and was grieved;
because thy word they failed to observe.

^{159}Consider how I love thy precepts: quicken me,
O LORD, according to thy lovingkindness. ^{160}The
summation of thy word is truth: and all
thy righteous judgments last eternally.

SCHIN

[161] Without a cause have persecuted me
princes: but my heart in fear
of thy word doth stand. [162] Upon thine utterance
I rejoice, as one that findeth plunder dear.

[163] I hate and I abhor untruth:
thy law I love. [164] Because of thy
righteous judgments, seven times
a day do praise thee I.

[165] Abundant peace have they which love thy law;
nought shall bring their fall about.
[166] I have hoped, O LORD, for thy deliverance,
I have also carried thy commandments out.

[167] My soul hath kept thy testimonies; and
them I love exceedingly.
[168] Kept thy precepts and thy testimonies have
I: because my ways are all in front of thee.

TAU

¹⁶⁹Let my cry approach thy face, O LORD: to me,
understanding give according to thy word.
¹⁷⁰Let my supplication come before thee:
deliver me according to thy word.

¹⁷¹My lips shall utter praise, when thou hast
taught thy statutes unto me.
¹⁷²Of thy word my tongue shall speak: for thy
commandments all are equity.

¹⁷³Because thy precepts I have chosen,
let thy hand be help to me.
¹⁷⁴LORD, I've longed for thy salvation; and
thy law is my felicity.

¹⁷⁵Let my soul survive: and it shall praise thee; and
let thy judgments help me. ¹⁷⁶I have gone awry
like a sheep that's wandered; seek thy servant;
for thy commands have not forgotten I.

Psalm 120

In my distress I cried to
JEHOVAH, and heard he me.
²Deliver, O JEHOVAH, thou my soul from
lying lips, and from a tongue of treachery.

³To thee what shall be given?
Or what shall be done to thee,
thou tongue deceitful? ⁴Arrows of the mighty,
sharpened with the embers of the retem tree.

⁵Woe is me, that I sojourn in Mesech, that
I dwell among the tabernacles of Kedar!
⁶My soul hath dwelt too long with him that hateth peace.
⁷I'm for peace: but when I speak, for war they are.

Psalm 121

I will lift mine eyes unto the hills,
from whence doth come mine aid.
²From the Lord doth come my help;
heaven and the earth he made.

³Thy foot he will not suffer to be moved:
he that doth thee keep
will not slumber. ⁴Lo, the one that keepeth
Israel shall slumber not, nor shall he sleep.

⁵Yahweh is thy keeper: Yahweh is
thy shade on thy hand right.
⁶In the day the sun shall not
smite thee, nor the moon by night.

⁷From all of evil shall the Lord thee keep:
keep thy soul shall he.
⁸Yahweh shall preserve thy going out and
coming in from now unto eternity.

Psalm 122

I was glad when unto me they said,
Into Y<small>AHWEH</small>'s house let us advance.
² Within thy gates, Jerusalem,
shall our feet assume their stance.

³ Builded as a city that's compact
altogether, is Jerusalem:
⁴ to which location do the tribes,
tribes of Y<small>AHWEH</small>, upward come,

unto Israel's testimony, thanks
to the name of Y<small>AHWEH</small> to submit.
⁵ For there the thrones of judgment, thrones
of the house of David, sit.

⁶ Pray for soundness of Jerusalem:
prosper shall the ones that cherish thee.
⁷ Within thy walls be peace, in thy
palaces prosperity.

⁸ For my brethren and companions' sakes,
Peace within thee, I will now declare.
⁹ By reason of the L<small>ORD</small> our God's
house, will seek I thy welfare.

Psalm 123

Unto thee I lift mine eyes,
O thou that dwellest in the skies.

²Behold, as eyes of servants look unto the hand
of their masters, and a maiden's eyes to the
hand of her mistress; so upon the LORD our God,
wait our eyes until on us have mercy he.

³Have mercy on us, LORD, upon us mercy have:
for exceedingly are filled we with contempt.
⁴Filled is our soul exceedingly with scorning of
those at ease, and with the haughty ones' contempt.

Psalm 124

Had it not been the Lord
 who was for us, may Israel now disclose;
²Had it not been the Lord
 who was for us, when men against us rose:

³then they had swallowed us
 alive, at time their wrath against us glowed:
⁴then overwhelmed us had
 the waters; o'er our soul the stream had flowed:
⁵then o'er our soul the waters proud had flowed.

⁶The Lord be blessèd, who
 hath not us given to their teeth as prey.
⁷Like as a sparrow from
 the fowlers' snare, our soul is slipped away:

· the snare is broken, and we are escaped.⁸Our aid
 is in the name of Yahweh; heav'n and earth he made.

Psalm 125

Trusters in the L<small>ORD</small> shall as
mountain Zion be,
which cannot be moved, but doth
bide eternally.

²As round about Jerusalem
the mountains are, so doth enring
the L<small>ORD</small> his people from henceforth
and evermore continuing.

³Indeed the rod of wickedness
shan't rest upon the just ones' lot;
so that unto iniquity,
extend their hands the just do not.

⁴Unto those, L<small>ORD</small>, that be good,
benefits impart,
and unto the ones that are
upright in their heart.

⁵But such as to their crooked ways
divert, the L<small>ORD</small> shall them expel
with workers of iniquity:
but peace shall be on Israel.

Psalm 126

¹ When the Lord reverted the captivity
of Zion, like the ones that dream were we.
²Then our mouth was filled with laughter,
and our tongue with shouts of glee:

then they among the heathen said,
For them the Lord hath done things great.
³Things great hath done the Lord
for us; we are elate.

⁴Jehovah, our captivity
revert, as in the south the streams.
⁵The ones that sow in tears
shall reap with joyful screams.

⁶He whosoever goeth forth
and weepeth, bearing seed to sow,
shall doubtless come again
with joy, his sheaves in tow.

Psalm 127

Except Jehovah build the house,
the ones that build it toil in vain:
except the Lord preserve the town,
the watchman waketh but in vain.

²It's vanity for you to rise
betimes, to sit up late, to eat
the bread of sorrows: for so sleep
to his belovèd doth he mete.

³Lo, children are an heirloom of the Lord:
and the belly's fruit a salary.
⁴As arrows in the hand of one of might;
so are sons of juvenility.

⁵How happy is the fellow that
with them hath filled his quiver: these
shall not be shamed, but in the gate
shall speak they with the enemies.

Psalm 128

¹ Bless'd is ev'ry fearer of the LORD;
that in his ways doth stride.
²For thou shalt eat the labor of thy hands:
happy shalt thou be, it shall be well with thee beside.

³Thy woman shall be as a fruitful vine
by the sides of thine abode: thy progeny
like olive plants around thy table. ⁴Lo,
the fearer of the LORD thus bless'd shall be.

⁵The LORD shall bless thee out of Zion: and
thou shalt see Jerusalem's prosperity
through all thy days of life. ⁶Yea, thou shalt see
thy children's children. Peace on Israel be!

Psalm 129

^{1} Abundantly have they afflicted me from my
youth, may Israel now say:
^{2}Abundantly have they afflicted me from my
youth: yet overcome me have not they.

^{3}The plowers plowed upon my back:
they made their furrows long.
^{4}The LORD is righteous: he hath cut
asunder cordage of the doers wrong.

^{5}Let disconcerted and repulsed
be Zion's haters all.
^{6}Let them as grass of housetops be,
which withereth afore it groweth tall:

^{7}which filleth not the mower's hand or bosom of
he that bindeth sheaves. ^{8}Nor do
the passersby say, On you YAHWEH's blessing be:
in the name of YAHWEH, bless we you.

Psalm 130

From the depths, Jehovah, have
cried I unto thee.
²Lord, hear my voice: unto the voice
of my pleadings let thine ears attentive be.

³If, Jehovah, shouldest thou
mark iniquity,
Lord, who shall stand? ⁴But there with thee
is forgiveness, so that feared thou mayest be.

⁵For the Lord I wait, my soul doth wait;
and in his word I hope. ⁶My soul doth stay
the Master more than they that for the morning watch:
more than they that for the morning watch, I say.

⁷Hope, O Israel, upon the Lord:
for mercy's with the Lord; with him, too, is
redemption plenteous. ⁸Indeed he shall redeem
Israel from all iniquities of his.

Psalm 131

¹ LORD, my heart's not haughty, nor mine eyes
lofty: nor do I
exercise myself in matters great,
or in things for me too high.

² I've behaved and quieted myself
surely, as a child
of his mother weanèd: even my
soul is as a weanèd child.

³ Hope, O Israel, in the
LORD from now and to eternity.

Psalm 132

L ORD, remember David, and
all of his afflictions: ²how
he sware unto the L ORD, he unto the
mighty God of Jacob made a vow:

³Certainly my house's tabernacle I
will not enter, nor up to my bed will go;
⁴I will give no sleep unto mine eyes,
slumber to my lids I'll not bestow,

⁵till I for J EHOVAH find a place, a tent
for the mighty God of Jacob. ⁶Lo, of it
heard we at Ephratah: in the fields
of the forest we discovered it.

⁷To his dwellings we will go:
at his footstool bow will we.
⁸Arise into thy rest, J EHOVAH; thou,
and the coffer of thy potency.

⁹Let thy priests be clothed with righteousness; let thy
holy ones moreover shout in jubilance.
¹⁰For thy servant David's sake, avert
not thou thine anointed's countenance.

¹¹Truthfully the L ORD hath sworn
unto David, not retreat
from it will he: Upon thy royal throne,
of thy body's offspring I will seat.

¹²If thy sons will keep my covenant and my
testimony that them I shall teach, then their
sons shall also for eternity
have a seat upon thy royal chair.

¹³For J EHOVAH hath selected Zion; he,
for his habitation, hath desired it.
¹⁴This for ever is my rest: I'll dwell
here because I have desired it.

¹⁵Her provision I will bless abundantly:
satisfy her needy ones with bread will I.
¹⁶With salvation I will clothe her priests:
and aloud for joy her saints shall cry.

¹⁷There the horn of David I will make to bud:
 I've ordained a lamp for mine anointed one.
¹⁸I will clothe with shame his enemies:
 but upon him shall his crown burgeon.

Psalm 133

Behold, how good and pleasant it
is for brethren to together sit!

²As the precious ointment on
the head, that on the beard cascaded down,
even Aaron's beard: that to his
garments' skirts cascaded down;

³as the dew of Hermon that
descended on the hills of Zion: for
there JEHOVAH charged the blessing,
even life for evermore.

Psalm 134

¹ Lo, bless JEHOVAH, all ye servants of the LORD,
which stand by night in the house of the LORD.

² In the sanctuary lift your hands,
and bless JEHOVAH ye.
³ May JEHOVAH, maker of the heav'ns and earth,
bless from Zion thee.

Psalm 135

Praise ye Yahweh. Praise ye Yahweh's name;
O ye servants of the Lord, give laud.
²Ye that in the house of Yahweh stand,
in the house's courtyards of our God,

³acclaim the Lord; for good the Lord is: sing
ye praises to his name; for it is pleasure.
⁴For the Lord hath chosen Jacob to himself,
Israel for his peculiar treasure.

⁵For I know that Yahweh's great; our Lord's
over all the gods. ⁶Whate'er did please
Yahweh, that he did in heav'n, and in
earth, in seas, and all the deeps of seas.

⁷Causeth he the vapors to ascend
from the earth's remote extremities;
maketh he the lightnings for the rain;
wind he bringeth from his treasuries.

⁸Who did slaughter Egypt's firstborn, from
human unto beast. ⁹O Egypt, who
sent within thee signs and wonders, on
Pharaoh, and on all his servants, too.

¹⁰Who smote nations great, and slaughtered kings
strong; ¹¹Sihon the king of Amorites,
Og the king of Bashan, too, and all
kingdoms in the land of Canaanites:

¹²and gave their land he for a heritage,
a heritage to Israel his nation.
¹³Lord, thy name's for ever; thy memorial,
Lord, is unto ev'ry generation.

¹⁴For the Lord will judge his people, and
pity on his servants will have he.
¹⁵Gold and silver are the heathen's gods,
of the hands of men the artistry.

¹⁶They have mouths, and yet they do not speak;
eyes have they, and yet they do not see;
¹⁷they have ears, and yet they do not hear;
yea, of any breath their mouth is free.

[18]They that make them unto them are like:
all the ones that trust in them are. [19]Bless
ye the LORD, O house of Israel:
O ye house of Aaron, YAHWEH bless:

[20]bless the LORD, O house of Levi: bless
YAHWEH, YAHWEH's fearers. [21]Blessèd be
YAHWEH out of Zion, dwelleth he
at Jerusalem. Acclaim JAH ye.

Psalm 136

Give thanks unto the L ORD; for he is good:
for his steadfast love endureth evermore.
²Give thanks unto the God of gods:
for his steadfast love endureth evermore.
³Give thanks unto the Lord of lords:
for his steadfast love endureth evermore.

·⁴To him who doeth wonders great alone:
for his steadfast love endureth evermore.
⁵To him that made the heav'ns with skillfulness:
for his steadfast love endureth evermore.
⁶To him that on the waters pounded out the earth:
for his steadfast love endureth evermore.

⁷To him that fashioned luminaries great:
for his steadfast love endureth evermore:
⁸the sun to dominate by day:
for his steadfast love endureth evermore:
⁹the moon and stars to rule by night:
for his steadfast love endureth evermore.

·¹⁰To him that smote the first of Egypt born:
for his steadfast love endureth evermore:
¹¹and carried out from in them Israel:
for his steadfast love endureth evermore:
¹²with both a mighty hand and an extended arm:
for his steadfast love endureth evermore.

·¹³To him which split the Red Sea into parts:
for his steadfast love endureth evermore:
¹⁴and through its midst made Israel to pass:
for his steadfast love endureth evermore:
¹⁵but in the Red Sea toppled Pharaoh and his host:
for his steadfast love endureth evermore.
¹⁶To him which led his people through the wilderness:
for his steadfast love endureth evermore.

¹⁷To him which battered great regality:
for his steadfast love endureth evermore:
¹⁸and terminated famous kings:
for his steadfast love endureth evermore:
¹⁹Sihon the king of Amorites:
for his steadfast love endureth evermore:
²⁰and Og the king of the Bashan:
for his steadfast love endureth evermore:

²¹and gave their land for an inheritance:
for his steadfast love endureth evermore:
²²an heirloom to his servant Israel:
for his steadfast love endureth evermore.
²³Who in our lowly circumstance remembered us:
for his steadfast love endureth evermore:

²⁴and hath redeemed us from our enemies:
for his steadfast love endureth evermore.
²⁵Who giveth food to all of flesh:
for his steadfast love endureth evermore.
²⁶Give thanks unto the God of heav'n:
for his steadfast love endureth evermore.

Psalm 137

There by streams of Babylon we sat,
yea, when we remembered Zion, we
wept. [2] Upon the willows in
its midst, our harps suspended we.

[3] For there they that carried us away
captive asked for words of song from us;
and our wasters asked for mirth:
A song of Zion sing for us!

[4] How shall in a foreign land we sing
Yahweh's anthem? [5] If forget I thee,
O Jerusalem, let my
right hand forget dexterity.

[6] If I don't remember thee, let my
tongue adhere unto the roof of my
mouth; if o'er my chief delight,
prefer Jerusalem not I.

[7] Lord, remember in Jerusalem's
day the sons of Edom; ones who said,
Tear it down ye, tear it down,
to even its foundation bed.

[8] O daughter of Babylon, who art to be
destroyed; he shall be happy, that rewardeth thee
as thou hast served us. [9] Happy shall he be that doth
take and dash against the stones thy children wee.

Psalm 138

¹With all my heart will praise I thee: to thee
I, before the gods, will carol tunefully.

²I will worship toward thy holy temple, and
for thy kindness and thy truth I'll give acclaim
to thy name: for thou hast magnified
thy saying over all thy name.

³Thou answeredst me in day when I did cry;
in my soul thou didst with strength me fortify.

⁴O Lord, thee all the kings of earth shall cheer
when the utterances of thy mouth they hear.

⁵May they also sing in Yahweh's ways: because
great is Yahweh's glory. ⁶High though Yahweh be,
yet regardeth he the lowly: but
the proud he knoweth distantly.

⁷Though I in the midst of trouble walk, thou wilt
me revive: thou shalt extend thy hand on the
anger of mine adversaries, and
thy right hand shall deliver me.

⁸Yahweh will perfect that which concerneth me:
Lord, thy lovingkindness unto ages all
doth continue on: do not allow
the works of thine own hands to fall.

Psalm 139

Lord, thou hast searched me, and me known.
²Thou knowest my downsitting and
mine uprising, thou my thought
from afar dost understand.

·³Thou dost fan my path and couching, and
art with all my ways familiar.
⁴For there's not a word upon my tongue,
but, lo, O Lord, thou knowest all of her.

·⁵Thou hast me beset behind and fore,
and upon me thou hast laid thy hand.
⁶Knowledge is too wonderful for me;
it's lofty, it I cannot understand.

·⁷Whither from thy spirit shall I go?
Whither from thy presence shall I flee?
⁸If to heav'n ascend I, thou art there:
and if I make my bed in hell, lo, thee!

·⁹If I take the wings of dawn, and dwell
in the utmost regions of the sea;
¹⁰even there thy hand shall me conduct,
and thy right hand shall take ahold of me.

·¹¹If I say, The darkness surely shall
cover me; about me even light
shall be night.¹²Yea, darkness hideth not
from thee; but as the day, doth shine the night:

as is the darkness, is the light.
¹³Indeed my reins thou hast received:
thou hast, in the womb of my
mother, me together weaved.

¹⁴Acclaim thee will I; for I'm made
terrifically, amazingly:
wondrous are thy works; my soul
knoweth that exceedingly.

¹⁵When I was made in secret, and
in nether parts of earth was wrought
skillfully, my skeleton
was from thee concealed not.

¹⁶See mine unformed substance did thine eyes;
in thy book were also ev'ry one
of my members written, which were formed
continually, when of them was none.

¹⁷And how precious are thy thoughts to me,
God! How great is their totality!
¹⁸Should I count them, they outnumber sand:
when I awaken, I am still with thee.

¹⁹Surely thou wilt slay the wicked, God:
therefore, bloody men, depart from me.
²⁰For they speak against thee wickedly,
thy foes uplift thy name in vanity.

²¹LORD, do not I hate the ones that hate
thee? Am not I also grieved with those
that against thee rise? ²²I hate them with
a perfect hatred: them I count my foes.

²³Search thou me, O God, and know my heart:
try thou me, and know my thoughts: ²⁴and see
if in me there's any wicked way,
and in the way eternal lead thou me.

Psalm 140

Deliver me, O L ORD, from the
evil human: from the man
of violence preserve me; ² which
in their heart do mischiefs plan;

together for hostilities,
they continually convene.
³ Their tongues they've sharpened like a snake;
'neath their lips is asps' venene.   *Selah.*

⁴ L ORD, keep me from the hands of the
wicked; from the man unkind
preserve me; who to overthrow
my progressions have designed.

⁵ For me the proud have buried a
snare, as well as cords; a net
along the wayside they have spread;
nooses they for me have set.   *Selah.*

⁶ I said unto the L ORD, Thou art my God:
hear, O L ORD, the voice of the appeals of me.
⁷ G OD the Lord, the strength of my salvation, thou
hast shielded my head in day of weaponry.

⁸ Accede thou not, O L ORD, to the
wishes of the reprobate:
do not promote his wicked scheme;
lest themselves they elevate.   *Selah.*

⁹ As for the head of persons that
compass me, let the travail
of their own lips them cover. ¹⁰ Let
burning coals upon them hail:

let them be cast into the fire; into
chasms, that they not arise again. ¹¹ Let no
evil speaker be established in the earth:
let evil hunt the vicious man to overthrow.

¹² I know that Y AHWEH will maintain the cause
of the wretched, and the right of paupers. ¹³ Give
thanks unto thy name the righteous surely shall:
before thy presence shall the upright persons live.

Psalm 141

¹ Unto thee I cry, Lord: hasten unto me;
to my voice give ear, when unto thee I call.
² Before thee let my prayer be classed as incense; my
hands' uplifting as the sacrifice of evenfall.

³ Set a watch before my mouth, Lord; keep the door
of my lips. ⁴ To evil things do not incline
my heart, to practice wicked works with men that work
wickedness: and on their dainty fare let not me dine.

⁵ Let the righteous person smite me; it shall be
a benevolence: and let him chasten me;
it shall be oil supreme, which shall not break my head:
for in their calamities my prayer shall still yet be.

⁶ When in stony places are their judges thrown
over, they shall hear my words; for sweet are they.
⁷ As one doth cut and cleave upon the earth, dispersed
are our bones across the underworld's entryway.

⁸ But to thee mine eyes are, God the Lord: in thee
is my trust; uncover not the soul of me.
⁹ Preserve me from the snares which they have laid for me,
and the nooses of the workers of iniquity.

¹⁰ Into their own nets let the ungodly fall,
whilst that I escape withal.

Psalm 142

· Cried I to J‍ehovah with my voice;
to J‍ehovah with my voice my plea
I made. ²Before him poured I out my plaint;
I showed before him mine adversity.

· ³When my spirit was enfeebled in
me, then knewest thou my thoroughfare.
Along the avenue wherein I walked,
they privily have laid for me a snare.

⁴Looked around I to the right,
and beheld, but none was there
that would know me: failed me flight;
for my soul no man did care.

⁵Unto thee I cried, O L‍ord:
Thou my refuge art and my
portion in the land of the
animate, asserted I.

⁶To my cry attend; for I
very low am brought: from my
persecutors rescue me;
for they're mightier than I.

⁷Bring my soul from prison, that
I may praise thy name: the right
shall surround me; for thou shalt
bountifully me requite.

Psalm 143

[1] Hear my prayer, LORD, give thou ear to mine appeals
in thy truth. And in thy rightness answer me.
[2] And come not into judgment with thy servant: for
justified before thee none alive shall be.

[3] For pursued my soul the foe hath; to the ground
he hath smitten down my life; in darkness he
hath made me dwell, as those that have been long deceased.
[4] Therefore is my spirit overwhelmed in me;

desolate my heart in me is. [5] I recall
days of old; I meditate on all thy toil;
I muse upon thy handiwork. [6] To thee I stretch
forth my hands: my soul to thee as thirsty soil.   Selah.

[7] Answer thou me speedily, LORD: my
spirit faileth: hide from me not thy
countenance, lest like unto the ones
that descend into the pit be I.

[8] Make me hear thy lovingkindness at
break of day; for I confide in thee:
make me know the way wherein I should
walk; because I lift my soul to thee.

[9] From mine enemies deliver me, O LORD:
unto thee I flee to hide me. [10] Me instruct
to do thy will; for thou my God art: good is thy
spirit; in the land of rightness, me conduct.

[11] Quicken me, LORD, for thy name's account: in thy
rightness bring thou out my soul from straits. [12] In thy
compassion extirpate my haters, and destroy
all my soul's afflicters: for thy slave am I.

Psalm 144

· Blessed be the LORD my fortitude,
   who doth discipline my hands for war,
   and my fingers for the battle: ^{2}my
   steadfast love, my fortress furthermore;

   my retreat aloft, and my
   rescuer; my shield, and he
   whom I trust in; beater down
   of my people under me.

   ^{3}What is man, O LORD, that thou
   takest cognizance of him!
   Or the son of man, that thou
   makest reckoning of him!

· ^{4}Man is like to vanity: his days
   as a shadow that doth pass away.
   ^{5}Bow thy heavens, YAHWEH, and descend:
   touch upon the mounts, and smoke shall they.

· ^{6}Cast the lightning forth, and scatter them:
   shoot away thine arrows, and them rout.
   ^{7}From above extend thy hand; me rid,
   and from many waters draw me out,

   from the hand of foreign sons,
   ^{8}whose mouth speaketh vanity;
   furthermore, their right hand is
   a right hand of falsity.

   ^{9}I will sing to thee a new
   song, God: on a psaltery
   and a ten-stringed instrument,
   praises I will sing to thee.

   ^{10}It is he that unto kings
   doth deliverance accord:
   who doth rescue David his
   servant from the hurtful sword.

· ^{11}Rid me, and deliver me from out
   of the hand of foreign progeny,
   whose mouth speaketh vanity, and their
   right hand's a right hand of falsity:

¹²that our sons may be as plants
grown up when a juvenile;
and our daughters corner stones,
polished in palatial style:

¹³that our garners may be full,
yielding ev'ry kind of ware:
that our sheep may in our streets
thousands and ten thousands bear:

¹⁴that our oxen may well bear
burdens; that there be no breach,
neither going out; so that
in our streets there be no screech.

¹⁵Happy is that people, that
in such way is situate:
yea, that people, for whom their
God is Yahweh, is elate.

Psalm 145

· Thee I will extol, my God, O king; and I
  will bless thy name for ever endlessly.
  ²In all the day, thee I will bless; and I
  will praise thy name for ever endlessly.

· ³Great is Yahweh, and one greatly to be praised;
  his greatness also is unsearchable.
  ⁴One generation to the next shall praise
  thy works and tell thy doings masterful.

· ⁵On the splendid honor of thy majesty,
  and on thy wondrous works I'll meditate.
  ⁶And of thy fearful actions' power, men
  shall speak: thy greatness also I'll relate.

· ⁷They shall gush the mem'ry of thy goodness great;
  and in thy righteousness they'll jubilate.
  ⁸The Lord is gracious, and compassionate;
  he's slow to anger, and of mercy great.

· ⁹Good is Yahweh unto ev'rything: and his
  compassions over the entireness
  of his creations. ¹⁰Lord, thee all thy works
  shall praise; and thee thy holy ones shall bless.

· ¹¹Of the glory of thy kingdom they shall speak,
  and they shall talk about thy mastery;
  ¹²to show to sons of men his mighty acts,
  and of his realm the splendid majesty.

· ¹³An eternal kingdom is thy kingdom, and
  through ev'ry generation doth thy crown
  endure. ¹⁴The Lord upholdeth all that fall,
  and raiseth all the persons bended down.

· ¹⁵Eyes of all upon thee wait; thou givest them
  their victuals at time appropriate.
  ¹⁶Thou openest thy hand, and satest the
  desire of ev'ry creature animate.

· ¹⁷Righteous is the Lord in all his ways, and he
  is holy in his doings all. ¹⁸To all
  of them that call on him the Lord is nigh,
  to all them that in truth upon him call.

[19]Fulfill will he the wish of them
that fear him: and he will detect
their cry, and he will save them. [20]All
that love him YAHWEH doth protect:

but all the wicked he'll destroy.
[21]My mouth shall speak the LORD's acclaim:
and all of flesh shall evermore
and ever bless his holy name.

Psalm 146

¹ Praise the Lord ye. Praise the Lord, my soul.
² While I am alive I'll praise the Lord: I'll sing
tunefully unto my God as long
as I still have any being.

³ Put not trust in princes, nor in the
son of man, in whom's no help. ⁴ His breath away
goeth, to his earth he doth return;
cease his thoughts that very day.

⁵ Happy is the one with Jacob's God
as his help, whose hope is placed in Yahweh his
God: ⁶ which made the heaven and the earth,
sea, and all that therein is:

which for ever keepeth truth:
⁷ which for them who are subdued
executeth judgment: which
to the hungry giveth food.

Yahweh looseneth the prisoners:
⁸ Yahweh openeth their eyes who lack of sight:
Yahweh raiseth up those bended down:
Yahweh loveth persons right:

⁹ Yahweh doth preserve the strangers; he
doth relieve the fatherless and widow: the
way, however, of the wicked ones
upside down inverteth he.

¹⁰ Yahweh shall for ever reign,
verily the God of thee,
Zion, unto ages and
ages. Praise Jehovah ye.

Psalm 147

· Praise the LORD ye: for it's good to sing acclaim
to our God; for it is pleasant; apt is praise.
²The LORD doth build Jerusalem: together he
gathereth of Israel the castaways.

³Healeth he the brokenhearted ones,
and he bindeth up their grievous maims.
⁴Telleth he the number of the stars;
calleth he to all them by their names.

⁵Great our Lord is, and of power great:
yea, his understanding hath no bound.
⁶YAHWEH lifteth up the humble: he
casteth down the wicked to the ground.

⁷Sing in giving thanks to YAHWEH; laud
sing upon the harp unto our God:
⁸who doth hide the heav'n with clouds below,
who prepareth rainfall for the sod,
who on mountains maketh grass to grow.

⁹Giveth he unto the beast his food,
to the ravens' sons which cry. ¹⁰In might
of the horse he hath no pleasure: in
legs of man he taketh not delight.

¹¹In his fearers YAHWEH hath delight,
in the ones that for his mercy wait.
¹²O Jerusalem, acclaim the LORD;
thine own God, O Zion, celebrate.

¹³For hath strengthened he the bars of thy
gates; thy sons within thee he hath bless'd.
¹⁴Peace he maketh in thy borders, and
thee he filleth with the wheat finest.

¹⁵His commandment sendeth he to earth:
very speedily his word doth dash.
¹⁶Yieldeth he up the snow like wool:
scattereth the hoarfrost he like ash.

[17]Forth like morsels casteth he his ice:
stand before his coldness can what one?
[18]Sendeth he his word, and melteth them:
maketh blow his wind he, waters run.

[19]Manifesteth he his word to Jacob, to
Israel his statutes and his judgments.[20]He
hath not so dealt with any nation: and as for
judgments, they've not known them. Praise JEHOVAH ye.

Psalm 148

Praise the LORD ye. Praise the LORD
from the heavens: in the uppermosts
praise him. ²Praise him, all ye his
angels: praise him, all his hosts.

³Praise him, sun and moon: him praise,
all ye stars of light. ⁴Acclaim him, ye
heav'ns of heav'ns, and waters that
higher than the heavens be.

⁵Let them praise JEHOVAH's name: because he gave
the command, created then were they.
⁶He hath stablished them for evermore:
he hath made decree which shall not pass away.

⁷Praise the LORD from earth, ye whales, and ev'ry deep:
⁸fire, and hail; snow, and vapor; squall
doing his commandment: ⁹mountains, and
ev'ry hillock; fruitful trees, and cedars all:

¹⁰beasts, and all the cattle; creepers, flying fowl:
¹¹kings of earth, as well as people all;
chiefs, and ev'ry judge of earth: ¹²both young
men, and maidens; ancient men, and children small:

¹³let them praise JEHOVAH's name:
for alone is elevated his
name; above the earth and the
firmament his glory is.

¹⁴Furthermore exalteth he the horn of his
people, praise of all his saints; of the
progeny of Israel indeed,
unto him a people near. Acclaim JAH ye.

Psalm 149

¹ Praise the LORD ye. To JEHOVAH sing a new
song, his praise in congregation of the holy ones.
²Let Israel rejoice in him that
made him: in their King let glad be Zion's sons.

³Let them praise his name in dancing: unto him
let them sing acclaim with tambourine and lyre. ⁴For
the LORD hath pleasure in his people:
with salvation he will beautify the poor.

⁵In glory let the saints be joyful:
let them sing aloud upon their beds.
⁶Let the praises high of God be in their mouth,
and within their hand a sword with double edge;

⁷to wreak upon the heathen vengeance,
and upon the peoples penalty;
⁸to bind their kings with shackles, and with
iron fetters their nobility;
⁹to upon them wreak the judgment written: this
honor all his saints have. Praise JEHOVAH ye.

Psalm 150

¹ Praise the LORD ye. In his sanctum praise ye God:
praise him in his power's firmament.
²Praise him for his mighty acts:
praise him to his greatness excellent.

³Praise him with the sound of trumpet:
praise him with the harp and lute.
⁴Praise him with the drum and dancing:
praise him with the strings and flute.

⁵Praise him on resounding cymbals:
praise him on the rackety
cymbals. ⁶Ev'rything with breath shall
praise the LORD. Acclaim JAH ye.

Appendix

Letters in Hebrew

Aleph	א
Beth	ב
Gimel	ג
Daleth	ד
He	ה
Vau	ו
Zain	ז
Cheth	ח
Teth	ט
Jod	י
Caph	כ
Lamed	ל
Mem	מ
Nun	נ
Samech	ס
Ain	ע
Pe	פ
Tzaddi	צ
Koph	ק
Resh	ר
Schin	ש
Tau	ת

Meters by Psalm

Psalm	Meters	
1	7.10.10.10	9.12
2	8.8.8.8	11.11
3	9.9	10.10.8.9
4	11.9.11.12	12.13
5	6.4.8.8	10.10.9.10
6	8.6.11.10	11.11.12.9
7	7.5.7.5	9.6.9.8
8	9.10.10.7	11.11
9	8.6.8.5	10.10.10.10
10	7.8.10.10	11.11.10.10
11	8.6.8.6	9.11
12	12.10.10.10	11.14
13	10.12.11.11	12.10.10.11.14
14	10.7.7.7	7.7.11.13
15	10.9.6.6	12.9.13.9
16	8.7.9.7	11.11.11.11
17	9.7.11.9	11.13.11.9
18	9.9.9.9	11.12.10.11
19	8.5.8.5	10.11.7.9
20	7.5.7.5	8.9.8.9
21	10.7.10.7	10.13.10.11
22	8.10.8.11	11.11.11.11
23	9.11.9.7	
24	11.12.10.9	12.12.12.13
25	8.9.7.9	11.11.11.9
26	9.7.9.7	13.9.11.9
27	11.9.10.9	14.13.13.11
28	8.7.7.7	7.8.9.11
29	10.10.10.10	13.12.10.12
30	7.7.7.8	12.12.9.9
31	10.9.9.9	13.12.13.11
32	7.8.10.5	11.10.13.10
33	9.10.10.10	11.12.11.12
34	7.8.8.9	9.11.9.11
35	8.9.9.7	11.9.9.11
36	11.12.12.12	12.14
37	8.8.8.8	12.11.10.11
38	8.5.8.5	10.11.9.9
39	8.6.6.5	9.9.9.9
40	8.5.10.7	11.11.11.11.12
41	12.9.9.7	13.11
42	7.5.7.5	9.9.9.9
43	8.8.7.7	9.9.9.9
44	8.5.7.5	8.8.11.11
45	9.8.9.7	11.10.11.11
46	9.11	13.10.12.10
47	7.10.8.9	10.9.8.10
48	10.5.7.5	9.9.9.9
49	7.7.7.7	10.9.9.11
50	9.7.9.7	11.9.12.10

Psalm	Meters	
51	11.9.9.9	12.11.11.12
52	10.9.10.10	13.13
53	11.7.7.7	7.9.11.11
54	7.7.7.5	
55	9.5.8.6	10.8.10.8
56	11.10.9.6	13.11
57	9.9.10.10	12.12.12.12
58	9.8.9.8	12.12.12.12
59	8.8.10.7	10.12.9.12
60	7.7.9.7	9.9.13.13
61	9.11.11.11	
62	7.8.7.8	11.9.11.9
63	9.9.8.9	9.11.11.10
64	9.9.6.7	10.9.13.11
65	10.9.10.7	12.9.8.12
66	7.7.7.9	11.7.11.8
67	9.8.9.8	7.10
68	8.5.7.5	9.9.9.9
69	7.5.8.6	11.10.10.10
70	8.7.9.8	9.9.8.9
71	8.9.9.9	11.11.11.11
72	9.11.10.9	13.12.11.13
73	9.9.10.11	10.7.11.7
74	8.5.7.5	10.10.9.9
75	8.5.7.5	9.9.9.9
76	8.7.9.7	9.10
77	5.7.7.8	9.9.9.9
78	11.9.12.9	13.13.12.12
79	9.9.8.6	11.12.11.12
80	7.7.9.9	10.11.10.12
81	11.10.12.10	14.14.13.14
82	8.6.8.9	12.10.9.11
83	8.8	9.9.11.10
84	8.7.8.8	9.9.11.10
85	9.9	9.13.11.11
86	8.5.7.5	8.8.12.9
87	11.7	9.9.12.11
88	9.9.8.8	9.9.11.11
89	7.8.7.7	11.11.9.9
90	7.8.7.6	12.10.10.11
91	11.9.8.9	13.11.11.11
92	8.8.8.9	11.11.10.9
93	6.7.6.9	12.14
94	8.9.7.8	11.9.11.9
95	8.5.8.5	11.10.8.8
96	9.9.9.12	9.11.11.11
97	8.7.8.7	9.9.12.11
98	9.8.10.9	10.13
99	5.6.7.5	8.9.9.7
100	8.7.6.5	9.7.8.7

Psalm	Meters	
101	8.6.7.5	8.8.8.8
102	8.8.12.10	12.11.12.11
103	9.10.11.9	10.10.10.12
104	10.10.10.11	12.12.12.12
105	7.9.8.8	10.10.10.10
106	8.9.8.9	11.10.10.11
107	9.8.9.8	11.11.11.11
108	9.8.7.7	11.9.11.9
109	7.7.7.7	10.9.10.11
110	10.9.11.13	12.10.13.11
111	10.9.8.7	11.11.11.12
112	10.10.10	10.11.12.12
113	8.9.8.7	9.11.9.11
114	8.7	12.11.9.7
115	7.7.7.7	11.9.10.9
116	9.10.9.8	14.11
117	8.11.7.10	
118	9.9.9.9	9.9.11.13
119א	9.6.8.8	9.8.12.9
119ב	8.8.7.7	9.10.7.8
119ג	9.9.9.9	
119ד	7.10.8.10	9.9.11.10
119ה	9.9.8.7	9.11.11.9
119ו	12.10.9.7	13.9.10.11
119ז	8.5.7.6	11.10.8.9
119ח	9.9.7.8	11.10.9.7
119ט	10.10.7.7	11.10.9.11
119י	10.9.9.11	10.12.12.12
119כ	9.7.7.9	10.8.13.11
119ל	10.8.7.6	12.12.10.8
119מ	10.10.7.5	8.9.9.11
119נ	9.7.9.8	10.12.10.10
119ס	8.6.7.7	12.10.9.11
119ע	9.11.9.7	
119פ	10.9.8.9	9.11.9.12
119צ	10.9.8.7	11.10.12.9
119ק	11.6.9.7	11.11.10.7
119ר	11.9.7.8	12.12.10.10
119ש	8.8.7.6	10.7.11.11
119ת	9.7.9.8	11.11.10.10
120	7.7.11.11	11.12.12.11
121	9.6.7.7	10.5.10.11
122	9.9.8.7	
123	7.8	12.11.12.11
124	6.10.6.10	12.12
125	7.5.7.5	8.8.8.8
126	8.8.6.6	11.10.8.7
127	8.8.8.8	10.9.10.9
128	10.11.10.10	9.6.10.13
129	8.6.8.10	12.7.12.9

Psalm	Meters	
130	7.5.8.11	9.10.12.11
131	7.9	9.5.9.7
132	7.7.10.9	11.11.9.9
133	8.9	7.10.8.7
134	9.6.11.5	12.10
135	9.9.9.9	10.11.11.10
136	10.11.8.11	10.11.12.11
137	9.9.7.8	11.12.12.11
138	11.11.9.8	10.11
139	8.8.7.7	9.9.9.10
140	8.7.8.7	10.11.11.12
141	11.7	11.11.12.13
142	7.7.7.7	9.9.10.10
143	9.9.9.9	11.11.12.11
144	7.7.7.7	9.9.9.9
145	8.8.8.8	11.10.10.10
146	7.7.7.7	9.11.9.7
147	9.9.9.9	11.11.12.11
148	7.9.7.7	11.9.9.11
149	9.9.11.11	11.13.9.11
150	8.7.8.7	11.9.7.9

Psalms by Meter

Meter	Psalms
5.6.7.5	99
5.7.7.8	77
6.4.8.8	5
6.7.6.9	93
6.10.6.10	124
7.5.7.5	7, 20, 42, 125
7.5.8.6	69
7.5.8.11	130
7.7.7.5	54
7.7.7.7	49, 109, 115, 142, 144, 146
7.7.7.8	30
7.7.7.9	66
7.7.9.7	60
7.7.9.9	80
7.7.10.9	132
7.7.11.11	120
7.7.11.13	14
7.8	123
7.8.7.6	90
7.8.7.7	89
7.8.7.8	62
7.8.8.9	34
7.8.9.11	28
7.8.10.5	32
7.8.10.10	10
7.9	131
7.9.7.7	148
7.9.8.8	105
7.9.11.11	53
7.10	67
7.10.8.7	133
7.10.8.9	47
7.10.8.10	119η
7.10.10.10	1
8.5.7.5	44, 68, 74, 75, 86
8.5.7.6	119ι
8.5.8.5	19, 38, 95
8.5.10.7	40
8.6.6.5	39
8.6.7.5	101
8.6.7.7	119ο
8.6.8.5	9
8.6.8.6	11

Meter	Psalms
8.6.8.9	82
8.6.8.10	129
8.6.11.10	6
8.7	114
8.7.6.5	100
8.7.7.7	28
8.7.8.7	97, 140, 150
8.7.8.8	84
8.7.9.7	16, 76
8.7.9.8	70
8.8	83
8.8.6.6	126
8.8.7.6	119ש
8.8.7.7	43, 119ב, 139
8.8.8.8	2, 37, 101, 125, 127, 145
8.8.8.9	92
8.8.10.7	59
8.8.11.11	44
8.8.12.9	86
8.8.12.10	102
8.9	133
8.9.7.8	94
8.9.7.9	25
8.9.8.7	113
8.9.8.9	20, 106
8.9.9.7	35, 99
8.9.9.9	71
8.9.9.11	119מ
8.10.8.11	22
8.11.7.10	117
9.5.8.6	55
9.5.9.7	131
9.6.7.7	121
9.6.8.8	119א
9.6.9.8	7
9.6.10.13	128
9.6.11.5	134
9.7.7.9	119כ
9.7.8.7	100
9.7.9.7	26, 50, 131
9.7.9.8	119נ, 119ח
9.7.11.9	17
9.8.7.7	108
9.8.9.7	45

Meter	Psalms
9.8.9.8	58, 67, 107
9.8.10.9	98
9.8.12.9	119א
9.9	3, 85
9.9.6.7	64
9.9.7.8	119ח, 137
9.9.8.6	79
9.9.8.7	119ה, 122
9.9.8.8	88
9.9.8.9	63, 70
9.9.9.9	18, 39, 42, 43, 48, 68, 75, 77, 118, 119ג, 135, 143, 144, 147
9.9.9.10	139
9.9.9.12	96
9.9.10.10	57, 142
9.9.10.11	73
9.9.11.10	83, 84, 119ד
9.9.11.11	88, 149
9.9.11.13	118
9.9.12.11	87, 97
9.9.13.13	60
9.10	76
9.10.7.8	119ב
9.10.9.8	116
9.10.10.7	8
9.10.10.10	33
9.10.11.9	103
9.10.12.11	130
9.11	11, 46
9.11.9.7	23, 119ע, 146
9.11.9.11	34, 113
9.11.9.12	119פ
9.11.10.9	72
9.11.11.9	119ה
9.11.11.10	63
9.11.11.11	61, 96
9.12	1
9.13.11.11	85
10.5.7.5	48
10.5.10.11	121
10.7.7.7	14
10.7.10.7	21
10.7.11.7	73

Meter	Psalms
10.7.11.11	119ש
10.8.7.6	119ל
10.8.10.8	55
10.8.13.11	119כ
10.9.6.6	15
10.9.8.7	111, 119צ
10.9.8.9	119פ
10.9.8.10	47
10.9.9.9	31
10.9.9.11	49, 119י
10.9.10.7	65
10.9.10.9	127
10.9.10.10	52
10.9.10.11	109
10.9.11.13	110
10.9.13.11	64
10.10.7.5	119מ
10.10.7.7	119ש
10.10.8.9	3
10.10.9.9	74
10.10.9.10	5
10.10.10	112
10.10.10.10	9, 29, 105
10.10.10.11	104
10.10.10.12	103
10.11	138
10.11.7.9	19
10.11.8.11	136
10.11.9.9	38
10.11.10.10	128
10.11.10.12	80
10.11.11.10	135
10.11.11.12	140
10.11.12.11	136
10.11.12.12	112
10.12.9.12	59
10.12.10.10	119נ
10.12.11.11	13
10.12.12.12	119י
10.13	98
10.13.10.11	21
11.6.9.7	119ק
11.7	87, 141
11.7.7.7	53
11.7.11.8	66

Meter	Psalms
11.9.7.8	119ר
11.9.7.9	150
11.9.8.9	91
11.9.9.9	51
11.9.9.11	35, 148
11.9.10.9	27, 115
11.9.11.9	62, 94, 108
11.9.11.12	4
11.9.12.9	78
11.9.12.10	50
11.10.8.7	126
11.10.8.8	95
11.10.8.9	119ז
11.10.9.6	56
11.10.9.7	119ח
11.10.9.11	119ש
11.10.10.10	69, 145
11.10.10.11	106
11.10.11.11	45
11.10.12.9	119צ
11.10.12.10	81
11.10.13.10	32
11.11	2, 8
11.11.9.8	138
11.11.9.9	89, 132
11.11.10.7	119ק
11.11.10.9	92
11.11.10.10	10, 119ת
11.11.11.9	25
11.11.11.11	16, 22, 71, 107
11.11.11.11.12	40
11.11.11.12	111
11.11.12.9	6
11.11.12.11	143, 147
11.11.12.13	141
11.12.10.9	24
11.12.10.11	18
11.12.11.12	33, 79
11.12.12.11	120, 137
11.12.12.12	36
11.13.9.11	149
11.13.11.9	17
11.14	12
12.7.12.9	129
12.9.8.12	65

Meter	Psalms
12.9.9.7	41
12.9.13.9	15
12.10	134
12.10.9.7	119ו
12.10.9.11	82, 119ס
12.10.10.10	12
12.10.10.11	90
12.10.10.11.14	13
12.10.13.11	110
12.11.9.7	114
12.11.10.11	37
12.11.11.12	51
12.11.12.11	102, 123
12.12	124
12.12.9.9	30
12.12.10.8	119ל
12.12.10.10	119ר
12.12.12.12	57, 58, 104
12.12.12.13	24
12.13	4
12.14	36, 93
13.9.10.11	119ו
13.9.11.9	26
13.10.12.10	46
13.11	41, 56
13.11.11.11	91
13.12.10.12	29
13.12.11.13	72
13.12.13.11	31
13.13	52
13.13.12.12	78
14.11	116
14.13.13.11	27
14.14.13.14	81

About the Author

Mr. Olson was born in North Dakota and resides now in Oregon. Other books by this author include:

Algebra and Trigonometry

Economics

Exercises in Algebra and Trigonometry

A Study in Romans

www.ingramcontent.com/pod-product-compliance
Lightning Source LLC
Chambersburg PA
CBHW050611100526
44585CB00034B/1073